A DEVOTIONAL GUIDE
TO HIS WRITINGS

Edited by
Gary W Deddo and Catherine A Deddo

THE DEVOTIONAL LIBRARY

GENERAL EDITORS: PROFESSOR JAMES B TORRANCE
AND DR MICHAEL JINKINS

SAINT ANDREW PRESS
EDINBURGH

First published in 1996 by
SAINT ANDREW PRESS
121 George Street, Edinburgh EH2 4YN

ISBN 0 7152 0720 2

British Library Cataloguing in Publication Data
A catalogue record for this book
is available from the British Library.

ISBN 0715207202

The Publisher acknowledges financial assistance from The Drummond Trust towards the publication of this volume.

Cover and **design concept** by Mark Blackadder.
Cover illustration adapted from George MacDonald: *Malcolm* (London: Kegan Paul, 1886).
Typeset in Garamond.
Printed and **bound** by BPC-AUP Aberdeen Ltd.

Contents

George MacDonald
Part I: *An Introduction*

George MacDonald
Part II: *Selections from his Writings*

Contents

CONTENTS

GENERAL EDITORS'
FOREWORD

THE editors of 'The Devotional Library' are pleased to present the second sequence of books in this important series designed to provide ministers, lay persons and students of theology with the finest devotional thought from great theologians. Previously the series has featured the devotional reflections of *John Knox* (by Henry Sefton), *Thomas Erskine* (Trevor Hart) and *John McLeod Campbell* (Michael Jinkins). This new sequence features *John and Donald Baillie* (David Fergusson), *Edward Irving* (Graham McFarlane) and *George MacDonald* (Gary and Cathy Deddo).

In a time when shops are crowded with books on spirituality and mysticism that sometimes fail to live up to their advertisements, we think it is valuable to return to deeper and richer well-springs of Christian devotional thought, to thinkers renowned for loving God with their minds. The authors of these volumes are themselves scholars intimately familiar with these Christian thinkers and appreciative of the spiritual life of the Christian. They provide in each book a lively and informative introduction to the life and thought of the theologian and an anthology of that person's devotional writings.

As one reads these classical selections, one may well come to a new and more radical understanding of what it means to be a 'theologian' – that is, a person who lives in and under the Word (*logos*) of God (*theos*). Indeed, these theologians encourage us all to discover our own 'theological' vocation, the call of Christ which comes to each of us to hear and receive with joy the Word who gives us life. Our prayer is that 'The Devotional Library' will provide its readers with a vast resource of devotional literature in the English language, so that we may learn what it means to live as Christians from people whose own lives have been shaped by prayer, reflection and response to this Word.

GENERAL EDITORS
Reverend Professor James B Torrance
Reverend Dr Michael Jinkins

ACKNOWLEDGMENTS

WE would like to thank the General Editors, the Reverend Professor James B Torrance and the Reverend Dr Michael Jinkins, for their invitation to prepare this contribution to 'The Devotional Library' series, and for their assistance in preparing the manuscript. Special thanks are also due to Mr Timothy Burbery for his careful comments and help with the manuscript.

We would like to dedicate this volume to all those who befriended us during our time in Scotland, especially those we came to know in the village where we stayed – Banchory, Kincardineshire.

EDITORS
Gary and Catherine Deddo
Princeton, New Jersey

PREFACE

GEORGE MacDonald was born in 1824 in Huntly, Aberdeenshire, Scotland. From that inauspicious origin he came to be regarded as one of the leading writers of the nineteenth century. While falling into relative obscurity within decades of his death in 1905, his influence has continued to spread primarily through well known twentieth century writers, many of whom regarded MacDonald as their spiritual mentor. Among those who were profoundly affected by his spiritual insights were G K Chesterton, Lewis Carroll, W H Auden, Oswald Chambers and, most notably, C S Lewis.

Those who have benefited from these Christian writers have inevitably been enriched through them by MacDonald. It was C S Lewis who lamented that so few were taking up his suggestion that his readers should also look to MacDonald for further spiritual insight since he regarded him as 'my master'. Indeed, Lewis attributes to MacDonald's fantasy novel, *Phantastes*, a crucial role in his own spiritual awakening – the 'baptism of his imagination' – which culminated in his conversion to Christianity. It is most likely on Lewis's account that there finally has been a strong resurgence of interest, both scholarly and popular, in MacDonald's work over the past decade or two, especially in the United States.

Throughout his life, MacDonald poured his spiritual insight into a wide range of forms as a Congregational Church minister, lay theologian, poet, novelist, story teller, writer of fantasy, private tutor, public lecturer, college teacher, literary critic, editor, correspondent, husband and father of eleven children. In all this he claimed to have only one calling: to announce the Gospel of the grace and love of God in Jesus Christ no matter what form his pulpit was to take.

MacDonald wrote over fifty books, five volumes of written sermons, two volumes of poems, dozens of stories for children, and numerous literary essays. Never completely forgotten in the academic circle of English literature, several of his short stories have remained classics. His two adult fantasies, *Phantastes* and *Lilith,* however, are widely regarded as his greatest literary achievements and deserving of special recognition for their contribution to the development of modern English literature.

The renewed interest in MacDonald is not based primarily on the literary quality of his work, but upon his profound and sometimes controversial illumination of spiritual truth found within it. It is these insights concerning the true character of God and human nature which lay behind all his writing and which have revitalised interest in him.

This devotional guide to the writings of George MacDonald lends itself to that growing interest. We aim to make many of MacDonald's most provocative spiritual insights as accessible for our thoughtful and prayerful consideration today, at the close of the twentieth century, as they were at the beginning of the century when MacDonald's writing first received so much acclaim.

GEORGE MACDONALD
Part I: *An Introduction*

As a writer, George MacDonald was well aware of the fact that whenever we read stories the meanings we gather are conditioned by what we bring to the interpretive task. Nevertheless, MacDonald was not cynical. He believed in the growth of the human soul through the grace of God. He remained wonderfully hopeful about the spiritual growth of even those who might seem least likely to progress. His conviction that we can grow to apprehend greater truth, deeper meaning and more profound goodness was not founded on some regularly observable and universally predictable propensity in humankind, but upon the character and purpose of the creating, redeeming, and glorifying God – Father, Son and Spirit. His hope in God's work, among us and within us, fuelled his imagination and breathed life into the many literary forms which his creative energies took.

We present these devotional selections in the same spirit and hope – namely, that no matter what readers bring with them to these readings, they may leave enriched and enlarged, renewed and transformed by the refreshing and healing waves of God's grace.

We stand in a considerable line of those who have been profoundly grateful for MacDonald's literary ministry. In the same spirit, we wish to introduce him to those not yet acquainted with his writings. We would also wish, for those already familiar with him, to extend once again the spiritual hospitality of his always restorative meditations through these selections.

As one of MacDonald's better known and self-proclaimed debtors, C S Lewis noted that the true greatness of any body of work is its power to evoke re-reading. He confessed that MacDonald's work had this effect upon himself. After many years of foraging among his more than fifty major works, we too have found that over time what he has to say, somehow, rings truer at each reading. We trust that these selections, although taken out of their larger contexts, nevertheless will not weary the well versed nor fail to provoke first time readers to consider MacDonald's thoughts and to investigate the completed works themselves.

Designing this edition of selections proved to be a greater challenge than at first anticipated. This was the case for two reasons. First, there exist a number of fine editions aimed at similar ends. Second, MacDonald's corpus is at once voluminous and eminently quotable.[1] Our aim has been to select those portions of his works that are both representative of MacDonald's key spiritual insights and most suited to providing for a sustained time of daily devotional reflection.

MacDonald has been criticised for being verbose and repetitive, and there is a certain validity to this charge. The style of his writing reflects to a large degree his age and place – Victorian Britain. More significantly, MacDonald takes a theme and explores it in great detail and depth, while accounting for many possible objections to his line of argument. He was attempting to provide careful correctives to certain formulations of the Christian faith prevalent in the ecclesiastical context in which he lived. Extensive treatment was also required by the intrinsic depth of the spiritual realities that he attempted to illuminate and by the limitations of human language itself. A cursory treatment of these themes cannot adequately do justice to his concern to call for a more profound apprehension of spiritual truth and even for a radical reassessment of convictions and attitudes which were at the time accepted as being absolute orthodox Christian faith.

To be sure, MacDonald does often circle the same territory many times, but from differing vantage points to provide a larger perspective and a more exact apprehension of that element of truth under discussion. Hence, we suggest that in many instances what have been regarded as digressions on his part are, in fact, prolonged meditations on various themes viewed from multiple vantage points. Such passages constitute the ruminations of someone attempting to get to 'the heart and soul of the matter'. It is just this material of his which best lends itself to us for our own devotional reflection.

Another equally important reason why MacDonald tends to dwell at length on certain themes is simply that what he sees he enjoys and believes is meant to be enjoyed by all. Certainly it is no grave fault for him to want us to stay in the presence of that which gives delight, to make time and provide space to entertain realities which are wonderful. In developing and restating in various ways a single idea, MacDonald invites us to take time to savour it along with him.

Consequently, most of our offerings are more lengthy unedited passages in which MacDonald takes the liberty to develop his thought thoroughly. In this way the reader may share more fully in these devotional meditations with him.

These selections are arranged around ten themes, with five to seven related meditations amplifying each theme. Thus readers may explore more thoroughly each theme, perhaps over the course of a week or so, and then take up another. Although the given order of the themes does follow the structure of MacDonald's theology, little will be lost if they are taken up in an order led by the reader's own interest.

The meditations themselves consist of selections for each theme of nearly equal proportions: first from the sermons, and then from MacDonald's novels. In the light of the fact that a number of writers in their treatment of MacDonald's thought have tended to consider his fiction – novels, fantasy, and fairy stories – apart from his sermons, it is our concern to point out that a proper understanding and appreciation of what MacDonald has to offer will be best gained by drawing together what he has said in them both.[2] Given his own declaration about the spiritual nature of his vocation as a writer, the acknowledged biblical source and norm of his insights, and the God to whom he regarded himself ultimately responsible, any interpretation of his work which either neglects careful consideration of his sermons (where he is explicit about his concerns), or the biblical texts and tradition within which he deliberately worked, will certainly jeopardise the possibility of receiving the best he has to offer us.

Given that this is a devotional guide, the selections are taken from passages that direct our attention to the reality and thus the basis and source of truth, faith and life as MacDonald knew it. The titles given to each of the themes reflect this focus. However, this selectivity is not unfaithful to MacDonald's own perspective, since even though the extracts are, by definition, not exhaustive, they are nevertheless central to all that MacDonald has to say and, perhaps more important, central to the kind of life in which MacDonald is eager for us to share.

HIS LIFE

An awareness of the dynamic religious context in which MacDonald grew up, received his training and exercised his ministry, is helpful in order to see MacDonald's contributions in both their practical and theological perspectives. This can also provide some correctives to the sometimes oversimplified and so misleading characterisations of his teachings (in either approving or disapproving directions).

Home

If the heart of the living God was the home George MacDonald cherished for both his essential nativity and ultimate destiny, then Huntly in Aberdeenshire, Scotland was his most proximate reminder of it. This was true especially while his own father, George Sr, was still alive at 'The Farm', as it was then called. It was there, and in that house which his father and uncle James had built, nestling between the hills surrounding the village and the River Bogie, that MacDonald spent most of his early years growing up. The family had moved out to 'The Farm' two years after MacDonald was born in the village of Huntly on 10th December 1824.

Despite his great love for Scotland, and Huntly in particular, from the age of 15, when he went away to Aberdeen to prepare for and then attend College, he lived away from Huntly. Yet he returned as often as he could, whether from Aberdeen or London, Arundel, Manchester, or even Italy. He experienced some of his most poignant regrets when his plans to return home were frustrated. One of the deepest joys of his life was when he was finally able, after many delays, to bring his new wife, Louisa, to see 'The Farm', to walk in the hills, stroll the streets of his boyhood and meet many of those to whom MacDonald had been able to introduce her only by means of his spoken or written descriptions.

Family and Father

The home in Huntly was shared by the families of George Sr and his brother James, with each one occupying opposite ends and sharing common rooms between them. 'The Farm' was home to MacDonald along with five brothers.

When George was not quite eight his mother, Helen MacKay MacDonald, died of tuberculosis. An emptiness overcame him which could not be compensated for even by the presence of his extended family. This tragedy was followed the next year by the death of his second youngest brother, John MacKay, not yet three years old. Four years later his closest brother, James, who was only eight years old, also died. During the seven years before his father remarried, his grandmother, always nearby in the village, came to play an even more important role in George's life both as an emotional and spiritual support. Margaret McColl, the woman his father eventually married, did however win his love and respect and he came to call her 'Mother'. He also became fond of the three step-sisters born to them.

Yet the loss of his mother and his father's seven years of single living certainly provided a rich opportunity for the affections of father and son to grow deep. Indeed, throughout his life George regularly confided in his father. This persisted, although his father would at times respond to him with a directness and strength that might strain most relationships. However, George was not disaffected, since there was an underlying and constant warmth which suffused their relationship. The quality of his relationship with his father contributed to his awareness of the wonderful character of his relationship to God, and Jesus' relationship with his heavenly Father. MacDonald's thoughts on this perhaps coalesce best in his 'Dedication' to the 1857 collection of Poems:

> *Take of the first-fruits, Father, of thy care ...*
> *Thou hast been faithful to my highest need;*

And I thy debtor, ever, evermore,
Shall never feel the grateful burden sore.
Yet most I thank thee, not for any deed,
But for the sense thy living self did breed
That fatherhood is at the great world's core.

Louisa – Pilgrim Partner

George met Louisa Powell through his cousin, Helen, and married her in 1851 after a decidedly romantic courtship lasting nearly six years. They grew to have an extraordinary love, founded on their strong and heart-felt faith and in response to numerous hardships they faced together. MacDonald was chronically ill with asthma, bronchitis and possibly tuberculosis, and on several occasions seemed near to death. His illness made it necessary for them to move house often and to winter and finally take up residence in Italy. They cut short speaking engagements and he was once forced to terminate the pastoral ministry of his congregation.

He and Louisa were never far from poverty and were rescued from penury more than once by his father and more often by friends. Income was nearly always generated by temporary sources such as his tutoring, freelance lecturing and writing. He had a steady income only during those few intervals when he was given regular preaching or teaching responsibilities. Louisa contributed financially to the family also. She tutored and more notably staged and eventually toured with the family as a drama troupe. The troupe put on different plays, with 'Pilgrim's Progress' as the staple of their repertoire. Even after MacDonald's name became well known, and he had no trouble getting his work published, his financial situation was never permanently resolved, since payment for it was far from generous. The fact that his novels were gratuitously pirated by American publishers constituted another injustice which left the MacDonalds in financial difficulty.

Louisa and George had eleven children. Additionally they took in an abandoned mother, her two daughters, and another orphaned boy. Family life for them was demanding but full and rich. He and Louisa lived to share their golden anniversary together. However, the happiness of their union had at times been over-shadowed by the pall of death. George endured the passing of all four of his younger brothers, and of two step sisters, one of whom died at the tender age of 14. George and Louisa out-lived four of their own children. One daughter died shortly after giving birth to their first grand-daughter who, shortly afterwards, succumbed to the same illness that claimed her mother. Needless to say, the death of his father, when George was 34 years old, tried him bitterly as well.

Throughout the years MacDonald desperately sought both to find for himself, and to extend to others, a true comfort when grieved by the death of loved ones. The most poignant of his letters undoubtedly are those of condolence. Although tested by such frequent bereavement, his trust in God's gift of eternal life nourished a genuine hope in the present which anticipated a glorious heavenly reunion.

Early Education

Although he grew up in a farming village, MacDonald's intellectual, artistic and spiritual gifts were recognised early and he was given an exceptional education to match them. His education began in the Huntly Parish School, taught by the minister of the Kirk. However, dissatisfied with the school, his father apparently set up another – the Adventure School – when George was eleven. Attending this school, with its high academic standards, meant that George's early education included Latin and classical Greek, mathematics and science. His ability to write metrical verse at an early age caught the attention of the schoolmaster. With strong encouragement from his teacher and father, George was sent to Aulton Grammar School in Aberdeen to prepare for entry into Aberdeen University. This would require winning a bursary based on a competitive examination. This he did, and he entered King's College in 1840.

The four year course included Greek, Latin, Moral Philosophy, Natural Philosophy, Mathematics and Chemistry. MacDonald developed a strong interest in world literature and took up German as well. He also took an avid part in the debating society and did well.

Spiritual Odyssey

MacDonald took his Master of Arts in 1845. His tenure at Aberdeen, however, proved to be a spiritually troubling time as he wrestled over gnawing questions regarding certain tenets of faith that were regarded almost universally throughout Scotland as orthodox. Thus he left his university training without a clear direction. Yet his struggles did not begin at college, but in his childhood. In *Weighed and Wanting* MacDonald reflected on these early questions:

> *I well remember ... feeling as a child that I did not care for God to love me if he did not love everybody: the kind of love I needed was the love that all men needed, the love that belonged to their nature as the children of the Father, a love he could not give me except he gave it to all men.*

Concerning his boyhood in Huntly, MacDonald wrote: 'I have been familiar with the doctrines of the gospel from childhood. I always knew and felt that I ought to be a Christian, and repeatedly began to pray, but as often grew weary and gave it up. The truths of Christianity had no life in my soul.'[3]

The character Annie in *Alec Forbes of Howglen* is undoubtedly autobiographical, revealing through her the response evoked in him by a certain kind of preaching:

> *The minister was reading, in a solemn voice, a terrible chapter of denunciation out of the prophet Isaiah; and Annie was soon seized with a deep listening awe. After the long prayer, during which they all stood – a posture certainly more reverential than the sitting which so commonly passes for kneeling – and the long psalm, during which they all sat, the sermon began .... He chose for his text these words of the Psalmist: 'The wicked shall be turned into hell, and all the nations that forget God.' His sermon was less ponderous in construction and multitudinous in division than usual; for it simply consisted of answers to the two questions 'Who are the wicked?' and 'What is their fate?' The answer to the former question was: 'The wicked are those that forget God'; the answer to the latter: 'The torments of everlasting fire.' Upon Annie the sermon produced the immediate conviction that she was one of the wicked, and that*

she was in danger of hell-fire ... when the prayer, the singing and the final benediction were over, Annie crept out into the dark street as if into Outer Darkness.[4]

During his time at University, George's brother, Charles Francis, and cousin, Robert Troup, both registered George's inner turmoil. Towards the end of his time at Aberdeen, MacDonald wrote to his father:

I am a Christian, though one of the weakest .... My greatest difficulty always is, 'How do I know that my faith is of a lasting kind such as will produce fruits?' I am ever so forgetful to pray or read God's word .... But I trust that if God has led me to Christ he will keep me there. My mind is often very confused. I have made more progress – much since I began to pray more earnestly for the Spirit of God to guide me. Pray that I may not be that hateful thing, a lukewarm Christian.[5]

Shortly after graduating from King's College, while working as a tutor in London, MacDonald spent hours by himself often reading his Bible. He wrote to his father: 'I love my Bible more. I am always finding out something new in it. I seem to have had everything to learn over again from the beginning – All my teaching in youth seems useless to me – I must get it all from the Bible again.'[6]

Looking back a year or so after leaving Aberdeen, MacDonald wrote concerning his spiritual journey:

And for a long time I did not seem to make any progress, though my more intimate friends perceived a change in me. By and by I became more in earnest. But I could feel little or no abiding joy in religion. I looked to myself and not to the atonement. All I had been taught in my youth I required to learn over again. In my distress I could only cry to God to help me, and often in the midst of it felt assured he helped me. I set myself in some measure to do what was right. I began to see some of the beauty of religion, some of the grandness of the Truth. I read my bible and continued amidst much that was evil in thought and behaviour to cry to God. My unhappiness compelled me to it. The Truth has been slowly dawning upon me. I have seen I trust that Jesus is my Saviour, though this has had little of the effect it ought to have upon me. I know I shall never be happy until my whole soul is filled with love to him, which is only a reasonable thing. I hope I am a Christian partly because in some degree I try to do the will of my Lord and Master. I wish to be delivered from myself. I wish to be made holy. My life is in God.[7]

Though full of questions and doubts, MacDonald did not abandon his search for a true knowledge of God; nor did he even decide to seek revelation from a source other than the Bible. Rather, he took upon himself the more arduous task of sifting through the preaching he had heard, and through his Bible, to discern the difference between human traditions and systems of belief and the faithful witness to the heart of the living God. This search led him to focus on the Gospels and the character of Jesus, and more specifically to the character of the relationship between the divine Father and Son carried on in the Spirit. It was here, in the loving communion, the oneness of Jesus with his heavenly Father, that MacDonald found the heart of God revealed, as well as the key to interpreting all of Biblical and Christian truth.

Like Calvin, MacDonald insisted that the will of God could only be understood in terms of his revealed character in Jesus Christ. Any attempt to describe God's will or ways which was not founded on this revelation of grace and glory was, to him, ungodly speculation. On this basis MacDonald worked through his doubts to arrive at a genuine faith; one that could not affirm the doctrines of double predestination, limited atonement, the priority of the law over the Gospel of Grace, the need for introspection to find evidences of one's election, nor a view of imputed righteousness that permitted Christians to lead lives of undisciplined disobedience in the hope that an externally imposed righteousness would be instantaneously deferred upon the elect at death.

In place of these arose – a vibrant love for God which anticipated his being drawn into an eternal communion with God, a desire to preach the Good News to all; awe of the holy and irrevocable decision of God to save everyone through Christ and by the convicting, converting and transforming work of the Holy Spirit, perfecting of them to become his sons and daughters; the desire for Christ-like holy obedience to the will of God; and a hope that what God had created in the beginning and had redeemed in Jesus Christ, would not be able to eternally resist the perfecting fires of God's unquenchable love. Given God's revealed character, MacDonald was not surprised that persons should receive life eternal, but rather found incomprehensible how anyone could, or why anyone would eternally resist the holy sanctifying love of God, at least once all deception regarding Him and ourselves had been removed by God. Thus MacDonald concludes his poem, 'The Disciple':

'Tis God I need, not rank in good;
'Tis Life, not honour's need;
With him to fill my every mood,
I am content indeed.

And if I ponder what they call
The gospel of God's grace,
Through mists that slowly melt and fall
May dawn a human face.

What face? Oh, heart-uplifting thought,
That face may dawn on me
Which Moses on the mountain sought,
God would not let him see!

Love was his very being's root,
And healing was its flower;
Love, human love, its stem and fruit,
Its gladness and its power.

I find his heart was all above;
Obedience his one thought;
Reposing in his father's love,
His father's will he sought.

*   *   *

And where I cannot set my faith,
Unknowing or unwise,
I say 'If this be what he saith,
Here hidden treasure lies'.

* * *

Lord, thou hast much to make me yet –
Thy father's infant still:
Thy mind, Son, in my bosom set,
That I may grow thy will.

My soul with truth clothe all about,
And I shall question free:
The man that feareth, Lord, to doubt,
In that fear doubteth thee.

Macdonald's Call to Ministry and First Pastorate

As we have mentioned above, upon leaving university in 1845 MacDonald did not have a clear sense of direction. While the ministry had been suggested to him, and though he was open to considering such a call, MacDonald leaned more towards a career in chemistry or medicine, having excelled in these while at King's College. However, the latter choice was out of the question due to insufficient funds to pursue it. His interest in going to Germany to study chemistry was also beyond financial reach. Consequently, he travelled to London to take up work as a tutor.

MacDonald became discontented with this temporary arrangement. He reconsidered the possibility of having a call to ministry. After consulting with his father, he decided to apply to Highbury Theological College in preparation for the Congregational Church ministry. MacDonald found the academic work stimulating but not fulfilling, since the teaching seemed abstract and lacking spiritual vitality. As he sorted through his own spiritual convictions, which had by then become much clearer, MacDonald realised that his own position was, in fact, somewhat heterodox, at least within the ecclesiastical context of his day. Consequently, he found theological affinity only with a small minority of clergy and theologians he came into contact with at this time. He nearly finished his course work, but did not complete the degree. Nevertheless, MacDonald sought an opportunity to take a congregation where he could preach the Christian Gospel.

MacDonald was aware of his precarious position and was uncertain whether any congregation would find him suitable. Finally, in 1850, a Congregational church in Arundel issued him an invitation to serve as their pastor. The relationship lasted two and a half years, a very short time compared to the norm for this era. MacDonald was never put on trial, but, after little more than 18 months, a vocal minority within the congregation pressured him to leave by reducing his already subsistence level salary by nearly a third. The greater part of the congregation, however, cautioned him to stop speaking on certain of his theological convictions such as, '"with the Heathen the time of trial does not cease at their death", which certainly implies a future state of probation'.[8] Mixed in with this formal request were suspicions about the influence of 'German theology' upon MacDonald, and his preaching regarding the dangers of accumulating wealth. Although he had many supporters at Arundel, he resigned the pastorate eleven months after receiving the initial warning, rather than cause a schism.

Clearly shaken by the experience, MacDonald questioned more than ever whether he would be compatible with any organised Church.[9] In fact, during his lifetime he did take one other church position, but this was terminated by a severe recurrence of his lung ailment which incapacitated him for months. Nevertheless, he took this initial experience as a sign that his primary vocation was still essentially to be a communicator of Christian truth, although henceforth his pulpit would merely take another form.

From boyhood MacDonald had a modest aspiration to become a poet and as an adult he realised that the Gospel was itself inherently suitable for being expressed in poetic form. When trouble at Arundel was brewing, he wrote to his brother Charles: 'I don't think I am settled here for life ... I hope either to leave this after six or more years, or to write a poem for the good of my generation. Perhaps both.'[10]

He also wrote to his father: 'Preaching, I think, is in part my mission in this world and I shall try to fulfil it. But I wish to raise a church for myself or rather to gather around me those who feel I can teach them to their profit.'[11]

Later, MacDonald was to be criticised for filling his novels with so much didactic material. His response to such charges was often repeated by his son, Greville: '"People," [George] once remarked, "find this great fault with me – that I turn my stories into sermons. They forget that I have a Master to serve first before I can wait upon the public".'[12]

Another criticism regularly levelled at George MacDonald is that his characters are idealised. His response, consistent with his sense of call and desire to serve, is voiced in *Sir Gibbie*: 'I insist that what ought to be presented ... is the common good uncommonly developed, and that not because of its rarity, but because it is truer to humanity ... [it is] the representation of a man trying to be merely as noble as is absolutely essential to his being.'[13]

MacDonald never gave up his high calling, even if it took primarily a literary rather than an ecclesiastical form.[14]

His Literary Ministry

George MacDonald produced over fifty literary works. He began with poetry, publishing *Within and Without* first (1855), followed by *The Hidden Life* (1857), a collection of his poems. He then produced the first of his two fantasies – *Phantastes: A Farie Romance for Men and Women* (1858). Subsequently he attempted a play, rewrote it as a novel, but could not secure a publisher for it. In 1860 he wrote a short novel, *The Portent*, for the Cornhill Magazine. At the prompting of a publisher, and in great need of money, MacDonald produced his first realistic novel, *David Elginbrod* in 1863.

Over a career spanning 25 years he wrote more than 29 novels, the realistic ones occurring within one of two distinct cultural backgrounds, Scottish and English. Combining realism and fantasy he produced the novel *Adela Cathcart*, where he presents a number of symbolic tales within a realistic framework. Later, he reworked this and extracted three of the best tales as separate pieces: 'The Light Princess', 'The Shadows' and 'The Giant's Heart'. Perhaps his best short tale is 'The Golden Key', which takes on mythic proportions.

MacDonald is perhaps most widely known for his children's literature. The three most familiar are *At the Back of the North Wind* (1871), *The Princess and the Goblin* (1872) and *The Princess and Curdie* (1883). Two other works written for adolescents are full length novels, the autobiographical *Ranald Bannerman's Boyhood* (1871) and *Gutta Percha Willie: The Working Genius* (1873). Before the end of his career, MacDonald's greatest work, the fantasy *Lilith*, was published in its eighth and final version in 1895. MacDonald himself regarded it as his only work which was specially inspired by God.

MacDonald also brought together five series of twelve or more written sermons, three of them entitled *Unspoken Sermons* (1867, 1885, 1889); the other two entitled *The Miracles of Our Lord* (1870) and *The Hope of the Gospel* (1892). He opens each sermon with a Biblical text and then explores its meaning frequently through a detailed exegesis of the Greek text and the implications for its interpretation. In these sermons MacDonald presents, explores and explains, in a careful, interesting and compelling fashion, his theological convictions. The sermons are dense but well-argued, and illustrated by Biblical examples and metaphors.

The points MacDonald makes, while founded on Biblical text, seek to find the ultimate source of the truths found there in the very heart of God present and speaking through Jesus Christ by His Spirit. Consequently the message he presents is never arid or abstract, but forthright, emotionally engaging and addressed to the conscience. He does not rehearse theological commonplaces readily accessible either to the inquiring lay person or even the Biblical scholar or theologian. The images MacDonald uses call for our imagination's highest and best powers to conceive of the awe-ful holy love of God present in the Word and illuminated by the sanctifying Spirit.

MacDonald's enthusiasms also moved him to lecture and write a number of academic essays on literary subjects. *England's Antiphon* (1874) is a history of English religious poetry from the thirteenth century to the 1870s, including explorations of 21 individual poets such as John Donne, George Herbert, Richard Baxter and Milton. *Orts* (1882) is also a collection of essays, the most important of which are two on the imagination, as well as pieces on Shakespeare, Wordsworth and Shelley. Last in this category MacDonald wrote a study of 'Hamlet', *The Tragedie of Hamlet* (1885), in which he presented an original and compelling interpretation.

In addition to writing, MacDonald found another literary outlet for his creative energies through regularly lecturing in Manchester and London. In recognition of his work he was awarded the degree of Doctor of Laws by Aberdeen University (1886).

He and Louisa spent the winter of 1872-73 on a lecture tour of the United States, on one occasion in Boston gathering an audience of nearly 3000 people. He became quite well known, although never reaching the popularity of fellow novelist, Charles Dickens.

MacDonald was in his day sometimes grouped by critics with such literary lights as Carlyle, Trollope, Thackeray, Macaulay, Wilkie Collins and Dickens. The MacDonalds were befriended by Victorian luminaries such as Lady Byron (widow of the poet), Henry Crabb Robinson, Charles Kingsley, Matthew Arnold, Charles L Dodgson (Lewis Carroll) and John Ruskin. The last two had a lasting friendship with the family. Dodgson was given the affectionate name of 'Uncle' by the MacDonald family. He modelled Alice after one of the MacDonald daughters and it was only after the book was given a well received trial reading for all the MacDonald children that Dodgson found the courage to have it published.

Thus, MacDonald was doubly enriched by being drawn into two frequently intersecting circles – one literary the other pastoral/theological. These two social spheres reflected the dual nature of his own spiritual vocation as preacher-poet.

The Fading Years of his Life

MacDonald's most productive years were those between 1880 and 1890, when more than 15 new titles were published, as well as several reprints. These included seven novels, two volumes of sermons, the second and third in the series of *Unspoken Sermons*, two collections of poetry, one of short stories, and two collections of literary essays. After this period of productivity his pace slowed. Nevertheless, he remained productive for the next eight years until he was 73 years old. He completed three more full novels: *There and Back* (1891), *The Flight of the Shadow* (1891) and *Salted with Fire* (1897). His last work was a novelette, *Far Above Rubies* (1898). Although these novels are not regarded among his best, in this last phase of his career he produced a final and impressive collections of sermons, as well as *Lilith*. *Lilith* is often regarded as the high water mark of MacDonald's literary achievement and indeed as a landmark in English literature leading the way in the development of the genre of fantasy.

In 1892 MacDonald began to express his awareness of a loss of vigour and stamina. The onset of his twilight years coincided with the death of his first daughter, Lilia, in 1891. Her death also had a devastating effect on Louisa and her health. Since 1887 he had suffered from eczema – the skin condition becoming so severe that it prevented him from sleeping. It was at this point, in the words of Greville MacDonald, that his 'brain sometimes would not respond to his imagination'.[15] MacDonald took up a discipline of reading and memorisation in the hopes of revitalising his mind. However, his sleeplessness made even his waking moments an agony. Louisa had to hire help to assist her in caring for George.

Finally, in 1899, at the age of 74, MacDonald had a stroke that left him virtually speechless, although his skin condition cleared and he slept soundly for the first time in years. He spoke scarcely at all for the final five years of his life, seeming to enter a silent vigil waiting for his final calling to enter eternal life and holiness in the presence of his gracious God.

He lived to celebrate his Golden Wedding anniversary in 1901 with many of the extended family present. Indeed, the comforting presence of Louisa seem to be the only thing which MacDonald noticed since his stroke. Exhausted and despondent about her husband's failure to recover, Louisa died in January, 1902. Two daughters, Irene and Winifred, were with her.

Fearful of the effect of this news upon their father, they delayed several days before telling him. When they finally did, George wept bitterly.

First Irene and then Winifred cared for him over the next three years. MacDonald died on September 18th 1905 at 80 years of age, at Ashstead in Surrey in the home of his daughter, Winifred Louisa Troup. Despite his wishes to be buried at Huntly, his body was cremated and the ashes were buried beside the body of his wife at Bordighera, Italy.

GEORGE MACDONALD
AS THEOLOGIAN

While MacDonald's most enduring power is his ability to communicate theological insight, he was not a theologian per se. He did not devote his life to the study of Christian teaching found throughout the history of the Church. Nor did he engage directly the highest levels of theological debate occurring during his life time. His own published thought was not comprehensive, in that he did not speak at all on many important theological themes. Thus MacDonald's treatment of the Christian faith leaves many issues and questions unexplored or only partially developed. When reading him, it is good to remember that the scope of his treatment is necessarily limited and not to expect all questions to be answered at the end of the day.

As a Christian thinker MacDonald exhibits an uncanny perspective; however, his treatment shows some weakness when his criticism of certain doctrines, as they were often expressed in his day, led him to reject them altogether. He seems unaware of the existence of alternative expressions of those doctrines that meet his objections and actually support his criticisms. Thus MacDonald rejected wholesale the doctrines of penal substitution and vicarious sacrifice without considering better formulations expressed, for example, by Irenaeus, Athanasius, the Early Church Cappadocian theologians, or even those written by Luther and Calvin. He was not nearly as careful a critical theologian as, for example, his contemporary John McLeod Campbell, although his criticisms and final conclusions are very much similar. MacDonald's position seems quite orthodox when it is seen in the light of the whole range of historically orthodox Christian theology, than when viewed against the background of his own particular theological milieu. Hence, his criticism continues to have great value for evaluating the claim to absolute orthodoxy of certain high Calvinist formulations of Christian truth widespread in his day and to a significant degree still influential today.

Although not without precedent, MacDonald has expressed Christian truth uniquely in a fresh and spiritually renewing way. In fact MacDonald's own theological formulations anticipated the theology of the Scottish theologian P T Forsythe (1848-1921), and perhaps more significantly, the magisterial work of the Swiss Reformed theologian Karl Barth (1886-1968).[16] The best known modern lay theologian, C S Lewis, acknowledged his unique and profound indebtedness to MacDonald and a reading of them both confirms the vastness of the theological landscape they shared.

The Living God and Theological Systems

MacDonald was in fact opposed to most of the technical or systematic theology of his day and would have objected to the label 'theologian' being applied to himself. He objected strongly to any Christian thinking that made the creation of a system the highest priority, so that the system itself became the criterion by which truth was apprehended. Such systems typically had (and have) a central controlling idea with which all subsequent beliefs must be logically consistent, and contain secondary doctrines which are generated by logical inference from that central controlling idea, otherwise having little ground for their assertion. In MacDonald's view, such Procrustean approaches often serve to eliminate the possibility of mystery or paradox.

Perhaps more perniciously, they tend to imply that it is our ideas or thoughts that are the primary realities accessible to us, thus obscuring the possibility of coming into contact with the real personal presence of the living God. MacDonald saw such systems as having a way of forcing themselves between the living God and his children, insulating them from participating in a vital communion. He regarded such theologies as human creations largely devoid of divine truth and thus felt that they should be open to question and even radical correction to the extent that they did not correspond to the reality of the truth of God in Christ. Such a critique was especially needed if theological systems served to create an abstract distance between God and his people. Thus MacDonald, along with his father, did not align himself with the dominant 'isms' of Calvinism or Arminianism, the two prevailing systems of theology in Europe in his time.

His rejection of systems of theology should not lead one to conclude that MacDonald devalued coherence or consistency of thought. Even if he exhibits a lack of theological precision at times, there is nevertheless a coherence and consistency in what he communicates. Although there is no controlling logical premise, there is a central reality – the revelation of the character of God in Jesus Christ. MacDonald speaks of a God who is present to us by the Spirit and as attested to by the Biblical texts. Even though he did not trust mere logical deduction to reveal the truth, he felt obligated to explain, interpret and even argue for the living truth of that which he was trying to communicate.

MacDonald, Biblical Truth and Controversy

George MacDonald was a minister, a preacher of the Gospel, as well as a poet, lecturer, and writer of realistic, fantastic and mystical literature. For him the Biblical texts were central and indispensable for all his writing and speaking, even in the realm of the imaginative and literary, because they were a faithful and authoritative source to lead us into the presence of God that we might 'enjoy Him forever' (in the words of the Westminster Shorter Catechism). Although he often does not use religious or theological language, nevertheless there is at the core of all his work a vision of the reality and truth of the character of the creating, redeeming and sanctifying God of Jesus Christ. In this sense then, we can say that everything he did was essentially theological; all of it was intended to be a sign of the living God.

MacDonald did indeed raise controversy in his day and his writing continues to do so. Some of the controversy arises on account of his lack, at times, of theological clarity. At some points when he writes discursively, he is not as precise or careful as he could be, even if only judged by what he says more accurately elsewhere on the same subject. A conclusive, fair and accurate assessment of MacDonald's beliefs requires a broad and thorough reading. Only then will one discover a complete picture of what he has to say on a given subject, see the connections between related subjects, and discern where he has best expressed his point compared to where he has put it less clearly. Such comprehensive reading is especially needed when considering how MacDonald understood the scope of Christ's atoning work, the relation of the transcendent to the natural and human sphere, and how he regarded the relation of truth and life to Christ and those who do not explicitly or consciously make that connection.

Likewise, care must be taken when attempting to ascertain the relative impact of the various sources of influence upon MacDonald. He freely explored the mysticism of Swedenborg and Novalis and even spiritualism (known then as animal magnetism). He was familiar with Plato, Plotinus, the Cambridge Platonists, and the German idealists Goethe, Schelling and Fichte, through his own reading of them and through contemporaries influenced by them (such as Samuel Taylor Coleridge and Thomas Carlyle). MacDonald was clear, however, that for him these philosophies never played a normative role, nor served even as secondary sources of truth requiring the harmonisation of Biblical revelation with them. The truth that might be found in sources outside Christ may be helpful in critiquing certain theological formulations of Christianity and for suggesting alternative forms for communicating the Christian message. But ultimately MacDonald believed that the norm for a true knowledge of God was found in Jesus Christ alone, to whom the Scriptures faithfully pointed, and apart from which there could be no true knowledge of God. If we are to be true to MacDonald's perspective, we should regard any secondary sources to be for him only subordinate and derivative of *the* truth found ultimately in God through Christ.

THE ECCLESIASTICAL
AND THEOLOGICAL CONTEXT
OF MACDONALD'S THOUGHT

In order to gain a perspective on MacDonald's thought, a knowledge
of the religious milieu in which he lived is invaluable for an accurate
interpretation of his theological convictions. Taking up this task
would require a book in itself. Most of the autobiographical and
literary commentary on MacDonald has been formed from within
a literary perspective by those with training in that field. However,
such works often do not reflect an in-depth knowledge of the
broader theological context in which MacDonald lived and wrote.
It seems to us that at times this has led to an over-estimation of
the uniqueness of his theological contributions, or to a misunderstanding of what he was trying to say. Understood within his
theological context, readers will gain a clearer perspective on
MacDonald's position within the larger context of historic and
orthodox (in C S Lewis's terms 'mere') Christianity.

The Religious Roots of the MacDonald Family

The MacDonald family's earliest religious roots were Roman Catholic.
However, after the defeat of Bonnie Prince Charlie at Culloden
(1746), MacDonald's grandfather, Charles Edward, aligned his family
with the national Church, the Presbyterian Church of Scotland,
recognised by the Parliament of Scotland and formed largely under
the auspices of John Knox (1505-1572).

Knox had been with John Calvin and brought the Reformation
to Scotland, which had officially turned to the Reformed Faith from
Catholicism by 1560. Both the Church of Scotland and other Scottish
reformed Churches in the end refused to be identified with the
Church of England (the Anglican Church) and so were all regarded
as 'dissenting churches', even though the Anglican Church was also
Protestant, ie dissenting, in the sense that it had separated itself
from Rome in the early sixteenth century. By 1733, however, dissatisfaction over the moral and spiritual state of the established

Church of Scotland became so widespread that a Secession Church was founded in 1733 with a more congregational form of presbyterial government believed to be more consonant with its spiritual vision. Leaders of the Secession Church sought the renewal of spiritual life and the evangelisation and conversion of people to a vital Christianity. Civil support and patronage for the Church were regarded as a threat to the vitality of the congregation. Differences of conviction over this issue led to its split into the Burgher and Anti-burgher factions (1747).[17]

George's grandmother had come to share in the general dissatisfaction with the established parish church and so attended, taking his father with her, the church in Huntly, the Missionar Kirk, which stood in this Anti-burgher secessionist tradition. A few years before the turn of the century this congregation had become caught up in a revivalism and their minister, George Cowie, invited the Scottish evangelist James Haldane to come and preach. This revivalism led to the minister's excommunication, although the congregation continued to thrive without a regular minister for the ten years after Cowie's death in 1806. Haldane had been rebuffed by the Church of Scotland for his evangelistic fervour and became, in 1799, the first Scot to be an ordained Congregational minister. Eventually the Missionar Kirk affiliated itself with this denomination. This was the kirk in which George Jr was brought up.

The High Calvinism of MacDonald's Scotland

Both the Congregational Church and Church of Scotland were Calvinistic in theological outlook, the latter regarding the Westminster Confession as the prescribed summary of Christian Biblical truth. Not all dissenting Protestant denominations in Scotland were of the Reformed or Calvinistic orientation. Some were formed out of a reaction to Calvinism which had its roots in a disputation in Holland beginning with a theologian named Jakobus Arminius in the 1600s. Religion in Scotland had inherited this perennial debate. The form of Calvinism predominant in Scotland during most of MacDonald's lifetime was shaped by its fourth or fifth generation of teachers since the Reformation. Although it had undeniably undergone some refinements and shifts in emphasis, it was nevertheless understood to be consistent with the teachings of the Reformers by most church leaders and teachers.[18] The terminology and theological framework used throughout Reformed Churches in MacDonald's day had for the most part crystallised by 1690 and for the next two centuries many of the ecclesiastical debates revolved around the same questions raised by that theological system. MacDonald found that he himself was compelled to wrestle with these issues.

The Calvinism of this period, known more specifically as scholastic Federal (or Covenantal) Calvinism, gives the central and controlling place to the sovereign willing of God to elect to eternal life certain individuals and in symmetrical fashion to reprobate others to eternal damnation. God has elected persons whom he wills to love in Christ and has reprobated others on the basis of his divine prerogative of justice as Holy Creator. Consistent with this theological starting point, the Law of God is understood to be prior to grace. Failure to obey the Law provides the grounds for God justly to condemn anyone to perdition. God's original and universal relationship with his creatures is understood to be conditional, so that condemnation is justified on the basis of a person's failure to fulfill God's conditions of a legally required obedience. Since all persons are God's creatures, all are bound to this contractual relationship. This legal arrangement is often referred to as 'the covenant of works' or 'the covenant of nature'.[19]

In contrast, it is held that the covenant of grace for the elect is established on a basis altogether independent of the covenant of works. It is not universal but limited, being established by the Son of God. Redemption is offered freely only to those whom God has chosen 'before the foundations of the world'. Often it was declared that even for the elect there must be a work of preparation. This was accomplished by first hearing the law of God preached. This was to result in one's conviction of sinfulness and being without grounds for God's salvation. The preacher must first do this 'law work' before he may go on to mention God's forgiving grace for the elect.

One further element in this strain of Calvinism should be noted. Since election is limited by God's eternal decree, the question inevitably arises as to how one may know whether or not he or she is of the elect. Much pastoral counselling involved assisting people with this very problem. A regularly offered prescription was called, in the Puritan tradition, the 'practical syllogism'. This took a number of different forms, but its essential formula was as follows: God brings to repentance those he has elected. If there is evidence of such repentance and a desire for holiness, with a deep heart-felt confession of sin, the doing of good deeds, or the termination of sinful habits, then it can be inferred that one is of the elect. Hence, careful self-examination for evidences of election was often encouraged. Those who prescribed such methods were also aware that such a method could never be infallible. It was debated even among high Scholastic Calvinists as to whether or not assurance of salvation, on any basis, was essential to the faith of the believer. The consensus arose that assurance was indeed not of the essence of faith and subsequently ministers who held the contrary position were removed from their pastorates.

MacDonald was especially troubled by these particular emphases in the teaching of the churches in Scotland. His own detailed study of the Biblical sources of the Christian faith, along with protracted interactions with a number of senior theologians of the church and colleagues, led him to the firm conviction that they misrepresented the heart and character of the God of Jesus Christ and the nature of the Christian life.[20]

Precursors to MacDonald's Criticism

In Scotland, a century before MacDonald's time, such a formulation of Biblical truth was called into question by a group of prominent ministers and laymen of the Church of Scotland, in what was called the Marrow Controversy (1717-1720).[21] Several Church of Scotland ministers – Thomas Boston, Ralph Erskine, Ebenezer Erskine and James Hogg – took issue with certain high scholastic theological formulations. James Hogg, in Scotland, republished the document 'The Marrow of Modern Divinity' (1645, in England) because it summarised well their own position. The General Assembly of the Church of Scotland issued what came to be called 'The Black Act' (1720) which condemned it. The Assembly faulted the 'Marrow' for teaching the following tenets: assurance of salvation is of the essence of faith; atonement is universal or unlimited; holiness is not necessary to salvation; fear of punishment and hope of reward are not proper motives for Christian obedience; that believers are not under the law as a rule of life.[22]

The controversy, however, did not disappear. Nearly a century later, a number of theologians and ministers, senior to MacDonald, desired to carry through these same concerns regarding the nature of grace, the scope of election, and the assurance of salvation. They objected in much the same way to those later formulations of Calvinist doctrine which had come to be regarded as the only acceptable orthodox formulations for the Church of Scotland. Perhaps the most notable of these was John McLeod Campbell (1800-1872) who was deposed from the Church of Scotland ministry after an ecclesiastical trial in 1831 for preaching 'the doctrine of universal atonement and pardon through the death of Christ, and also the doctrine that assurance is of the essence of faith and necessary to salvation'.[23]

During MacDonald's university days a controversy broke out in Glasgow within the divinity faculty over the teaching of the doctrine of Universal Redemption by the United Secession Church minister James Morison, the founder of the Evangelical Union (1843). The debate spread and had an effect upon MacDonald and some of his classmates who were attending with him Blackfriars Congregational Church in Aberdeen.

Others were at the same time also expressing a conviction sympathetic to McLeod Campbell's. McLeod Campbell knew and corresponded with two other Scots – the lay theologian Thomas Erskine of Linlathen (1788-1870) and the minister of the National Scotch Church, London, Edward Irving (1792-1834) – who shared similar views on Christ's atonement. George MacDonald's personal connection to these three was made through the theologian and minister, A J Scott, whom he came to regard as his own spiritual mentor. Scott was well acquainted with McLeod Campbell and Irving, having been pastoral assistant to McLeod Campbell in his church near Glasgow and later to Irving in London. He also met Erskine in 1865. Scott is known to have shared to a large degree the theology of these three. MacDonald's own position was probably closest to Scott's, but since Scott did little writing we have no detailed record of his teachings. However, a comparison of MacDonald's teaching with that of McLeod Campbell, shows a great deal of similarity on crucial theological issues such as our essential filial, rather than legal, relation to God and the nature of the atonement. MacDonald also had personal contact with Thomas Erskine who likewise was well acquainted with McLeod Campbell. The theology of MacDonald and Erskine on the Fatherhood of God, the nature of the atonement and the doctrine of election are also largely in agreement.

George MacDonald also highly regarded, and was befriended by, the theologian and preacher F D Maurice (1805-1872) who also spent time with Thomas Erskine. MacDonald benefited greatly from his ministry and teaching, and especially appreciated Maurice's concern for the urban poor and family life. However, a comparison of their teachings reveals that while they had much in common, MacDonald, on some central points, diverged from the accepted orthodox perspective and emphasis less than Maurice, and was closer to McLeod Campbell, Erskine and Irving.

MacDonald's Unique Contribution

Thus MacDonald's set of objections to high federal Calvinism in theological content was not unique in his time nor without historical precedent. What is significant about MacDonald is his presentation of the issues, especially in his sermons where he at once demonstrates a Biblical and theological integrity, shows clear argumentation, all the while maintaining an impressive lucidity and concreteness. Hence, his thought is vivid and accessible to the layman, especially in comparison to McLeod Campbell's frequently difficult style, or the more technical theology produced by others. Moreover, MacDonald's contribution is original because he has embodied it uniquely and powerfully in a variety of literary forms including poetry, parable, ballad, fantasy, fairy tale and novel. His ability to communicate to his audience his Christian convictions in dynamic and imaginatively engaging ways stand as his greatest gift.

As we have suggested above, his biblical and theological teaching and fictional writings are both best grasped and appreciated when viewed stereoscopically. In other words, as C S Lewis has pointed out, the true value of what MacDonald has to offer lies in his unique combination of theological truth and literary art, not in either part taken alone. Thus the importance of MacDonald's work is not in its uniqueness of content, but in his compelling formulation of an ongoing theological critique against high Scholastic and federal Calvinism, and his own development of essential Christian truth which he powerfully expresses with a unique clarity, concreteness and creativity.

CONCLUSION

We have attempted in the first part of this volume to provide a concise introduction, contributing at least towards deflecting any unnecessary and distracting misunderstandings or unwarranted interpretations. In this way the careful and concerned reader may be guided through this arrangement and selection of the material presented here, hopefully gaining a fair perspective on what MacDonald presents and being able to take away the best that he has to offer.

Today, interest in MacDonald's writing is increasing, particularly among those who share his love for the harmony of the two spheres of Christian faith and literature. C S Lewis argued that, although from a literary perspective MacDonald can be faulted on a number of counts, even so, those who love holiness, MacDonald and perhaps Scotland too, 'can find even in the worst of them something that disarms criticism and will come to feel a queer, awkward charm in their very faults'.[24]

We, the editors, have come to revere MacDonald through a growing acquaintance with his writings over the years. We are convinced that MacDonald has also played an important part in our own spiritual journeys by assisting us to draw closer to the God of loving holiness. It is our hope and prayer that, for all who read it, this volume might somehow contribute to a greater appreciation of MacDonald. But, most importantly, that it might lead to a deeper awareness of the holy goodness of God's character and a more profound devotion to the God of our Lord Jesus Christ. A devotion which reflects George MacDonald's – one which overflows into a living hope for an eternal union and communion in the great heart of our faithful God, Father, Son and Holy Spirit.

Notes to Text

1   MacDonald wrote out a daily devotional book, a series of 366 sonnets entitled: *Diary of An Old Soul.* C S Lewis has compiled an excellent anthology which traces its way through many of MacDonald's writings, excerpting mostly short sections for consideration. More recently selections have been compiled and edited by David L Neuhouser, another by Michael Phillips, and most recently one by Rolland Hein. Also available are edited versions of a number of his sermons, most notably, three by Rolland Hein. (See 'A Select Bibliographical Guide', below.)

2   Indeed, some have noted that what sets MacDonald apart from nearly every other Victorian writer is that his novels might be classified as theological romances, giving them a unique power and intrigue. Clearly, the supernatural element of his fantasies and fairy stories is ordered by a Christian sense of the good and wariness of the subtleties of evil. C S Lewis has pointed this out most clearly when, in an auto-biographical section of his book *The Great Divorce*, the narrator declares his gratitude to his heavenly guide, who is no other than George MacDonald: 'I tried, trembling, to tell this man all that his writings had done for me. I tried to tell how a certain frosty afternoon at Leatherhead Station when I first bought a copy of *Phantastes* (being then about sixteen years old) had been to me what the first sight of Beatrice had been to Dante: Here begins the New Life. I started to confess how long that Life had delayed in the region of imagination merely: how slowly and reluctantly I had come to admit that his Christendom had more than an accidental connexion with it, how hard I had tried not to see that the true name of the quality which first met me in his books is Holiness' (p 65). Any attempt to understand MacDonald's exultation in nature, his rapture of human love, or his fascination with the supernatural, that is, his Romanticism, while dismissing his Christian theological orientation, will miss the essence of what he has to offer.

3   From his application to Highbury Theological College, 8th August 1848, in Dr Williams Library, Gordon Square, London. Quoted in William Raeper: *George MacDonald* (Lion Publishing Co: Tring, Batavia, Sydney, 1987), p 38.

4   *Alec Forbes*, vol I, pp 232-236.

5   GMD to GMD Sr, 8th November, 1845, Yale – quoted in Raeper: p 58.

6   Greville MacDonald: *George MacDonald and His Wife* (GMAW) (London, 1924), p 108.

7   From his application to Highbury Theological College, 8th August 1848, quoted in Raeper: pp 53-54.

8   GMAW, p 180.

9   MacDonald eventually became a member of the Anglican Church, but did not pursue ordination within it.

10   Letter, GMD to Charles Francis MacDonald, 4th November 1850 (ALS Yale), quoted in Raeper: p 80.

11   To his father, 6th February, 17th October 1853 (ALS Yale), quoted in Raeper: pp 98, 99.

12   GMAW, p 375.

13   C S Lewis has few complaints about MacDonald's preaching or good characters, but rather thinks it a strength. Of MacDonald's characters, he said they are 'highly idealized – Yet somehow they convince me. Or if they don't quite convince me as real people, they differ from most ideal characters in this, that I wish they *were* real' (January 17th 1931, letter to Greeves in Walter Hooper (ed): *They Stand Together, The Letters of C S Lewis to Arthur Greeves* (TST) (1914-1963) (Macmillan: New York, 1979), p 403.

    About the novel *What's Mine's Mine*, Lewis remarked, 'it is good not despite, but because of, its preaching – or rather (preaching is a bad word) its spiritual knowledge. So many clever writers strike one as quite childish after MacDonald: they seem not even to have begun to understand so many things' (February 23rd 1931, letter to Greeves [TST, p 407]). In another letter (August 31st 1930 [TST, p 389]), Lewis sums up his appreciation of MacDonald: 'I know nothing that gives me such a feeling of spiritual healing, of being washed, as to read G MacDonald.'

14   'Once more I asked him why he did not, for change and variety, write a story of mere human passion and artistic plot. He replied that he would like to write it. I asked him further whether his highest literary quality was not in a measure injured by what must seem to many

the monotony of his theme – referring to the novels alone. He admitted that it was possible; and went on to tell me that, having begun to do his work as a congregational minister, and having been driven ... into giving up the professional pulpit, he was no less impelled than compelled to use unceasingly the new platform whence he had found that his voice could carry so far' – R. MacDonald: 'George MacDonald: A Personal Note', in Frederick Watson (ed): *From a Northern Window* (London, 1911), p 67.

15 GMAW, p 558.

16 Most notable is MacDonald's grasp of the 'humanity of God' which anticipates the theme developed in Karl Barth's mature thinking, using the identical phraseology. See MacDonald: 'The Resurrection' in *Miracles,* p 265; 'Creation in Christ' (Series 3) in *Unspoken Sermons*, p 15; 'Mirrors of the Lord', p 52; and Karl Barth: 'The Humanity of God' in *The Humanity of God* (John Knox Press: Atlanta, 1974); and also *Church Dogmatics*, III.2.44 (T&T Clark: Edinburgh, 1960).

Other significant parallels between the two involve the essence of God being sovereign love, not will or power, the full personal revelation of the Father by the Son, the conjoining of act and being in God and humanity, the self-enactment of persons as a reflection of the freedom of God, the deceitful emptiness and impotence of evil, the priority of grace even in God's wrath, the personal and eternal communion of the Triune God.

17 The latter group was opposed to ministers taking the oath required of burgesses in some cities by which they pledged to uphold true religion as defined by the laws of Scotland. This was seen by them as an entanglement with the established Church.

18 The debate still continues today as to whether or not the re-formulation of Reformation theology by second and third generation Calvinists of Scotland such as Samuel Rutherford (1600-1661), David Dickson, or in England earlier by Dudley Fenner, Thomas Cartwright and William Perkins, and which was generally codified in the *Westminster Confession* (1643-46) and the accompanying *Sum of Saving Knowledge* (1650) was continuous with or was in some significant ways a departure from Calvin (and Knox) and Biblical teaching as Calvin had interpreted it. The central controversies involve the proper emphasis and role of the sovereign decrees of God regarding the doctrine election, the viability of the doctrine of double predestination (that is, of persons being predestinated for both election and reprobation), and the scope of Christ's atoning work. MacDonald distinguished between Calvin's

teachings and that of many of those who followed after him, and judged that there was a significant discontinuity between them.

'They take up what their leader, urged by the necessity of the time, spoke loudest, never heeding what he loved most; and then work the former out to a logical perdition of everything belonging to the latter' (*David Elginbrod*, vol 1, p 93). Comparing MacDonald with theologians historically, his thought, especially concerning the role of the incarnation and the relationship of the Father and Son for our knowledge of God, is most like Athanasius, the Cappadocian Fathers (Gregory Nazianzus, Gregory of Nyssa and Basil of Caesarea), and Hilary of Poitiers. There are also similarities between his thought and the writings of Richard of St Victor.

Although George MacDonald lacks their precision and theological breadth, some modern and contemporary writers with whom MacDonald has affinities are C S Lewis, the theologians Donald Bloesch, Alasdair Heron, James B Torrance, Thomas F Torrance, and also Karl Barth.

19   The terminology of 'covenant of works' applied to all humanity on the basis of God's relationship with Adam has been traced back to its first articulation in Germany proposed by Zacharias Ursinus in 1561-62. It did not become a theological commonplace until after 1584, twenty years after Calvin's death. See David A Weir: *The Origins of the Federal Theology in the Sixteenth-Century Reformation Thought* (Clarendon Press: Oxford, 1990).

20   While others shared with MacDonald in their critique of these strands in Calvinism, they often concluded by reducing the character of God to an indulgent kindness and the Christian faith to the ethical teachings or religious consciousness of Jesus. MacDonald's view differs radically from these 'liberal' conclusions. He upholds God's majesty and holiness and his loving purpose to perfect and make holy his beloved creatures through the atoning work of Jesus Christ, the Son of God. This, in MacDonald's view, inevitably calls for the repentance, conversion and transformation of all persons into the holy and loving likeness of Jesus Christ. Without this conversion and sanctification, no one can know the blessedness of living eternally in God's loving presence. Given God's character as made known in Jesus Christ, what is beyond understanding, for MacDonald, is how or why anyone could or would want to eternally resist such holy love.

21   None of MacDonald's primary biographers seem to be adequately aware of this theological context. While MacDonald's theological

position is unique among Scottish and English writers of the time who had rejected Calvinism, as G K Chesterton points out, it is not so original when compared to the writing and teaching of others in the theological arena of his day or the generation before him. MacDonald benefited from his personal and, in some cases, extended communication with others, most of them his seniors, who were agonising over similar questions and arriving at similar positions, sometimes at high personal cost. With the help of such high recommendation given by C S Lewis to MacDonald's literary genius and power of expression, his alternative to high scholastic Federal Calvinism has become today far more widely known. Even if his theological ideas at times lack precision, are open to misunderstanding at some points, and could be better and more fully developed theologically, taken as a whole his contribution is invaluable to anyone seeking to work though these theological issues on a biblical and Christ-centred basis.

22   See Charles Bell: *Calvin and Scottish Theology. The Doctrine of Assurance* (Handsel Press: Edinburgh, 1985).

23   Presbytery records quoted by J D Douglass: 'Campbell, John McLeod', *The Dictionary of the Christian Church* (Grand Rapids: Zondervan, 1981), p 185.

24   C S Lewis: *George MacDonald, An Anthology*, p xxix.

A SELECT BIBLIOGRAPHICAL GUIDE

While many of his short children's stories are readily available, unedited editions of George MacDonald's novels, sermons, poems and essays are difficult to locate. Slowly more of his literary works and sermons are being re-published, most often as reprints. The information below is provided to help the reader to locate the re-publications and reprints of MacDonald's original works now available and also to find edited versions of his work. Also included are select secondary sources about MacDonald and his writings.

BOOKS ABOUT GEORGE MACDONALD

Greville MacDonald: *George MacDonald and His Wife* (Unwin and Allen: London, 1924). (Also by Johnson Reprint Corporation.)

William Raeper: *George MacDonald* (Lion Publishing Co: Tring, Batavia, Sydney, 1987).

David S Robb: *George MacDonald* (Scottish Academic Press: Edinburgh, 1987).

Rolland Hein: *The Harmony Within, The Spiritual Vision of George MacDonald* (Wm B Eerdmans: Grand Rapids, 1982).

Michael R Phillips: *George MacDonald, Scotland's Beloved Storyteller* (Bethany House Publishers: Minneapolis, 1987).

Elizabeth Saintsbury: *George MacDonald – A Short Life* (Canongate Publishing Ltd: Edinburgh, 1987).

ANTHOLOGIES

C S Lewis: *George MacDonald, An Anthology* (Macmillan: New York, 1978).

Rolland Hein (ed): *The World of George MacDonald: An Anthology of Selections from the Novels* (Harold Shaw Publishers: Wheaton, Illinois, 1978).

Rolland Hein (ed): *The Heart of George MacDonald* (Harold Shaw Publishers: Wheaton, Illinois, 1994).

David Neuhouser (ed): *George MacDonald, Selections from his Greatest Works* (Victor Books, 1990).

Michael R Phillips: *George MacDonald, Discovering the Character of God* (Bethany House Publishers: Minneapolis, 1989).

RE-PUBLICATIONS AND REPRINTS

Facsimile reprints of the first editions of all five of George MacDonald's sermon series, listed below, are available from J Joseph Flynn, 2220 Mandeville Canyon Road, Los Angeles, California, 90049, USA:

Unspoken Sermons, Series One, Two and Three
The Hope of the Gospel
The Miracles of our Lord

Lilith is published by Wm B Eerdmans, Grand Rapids, USA.
Phantastes is published by Wm B Eerdmans, USA.
Diary of an Old Soul is published by Augsburg Publishing House, Minneapolis, Minnesota, USA.

Reprints of more than three dozen of MacDonald's novels and fantasies are available from: Johannesen Printing and Publishing, PO Box 24, Whitethorn, California, 95589, USA. UK Distributor: Rachel Johnson, 61 Longdales Road, Lincoln LN2 2JS – (Tel) 01522 532 967.

Edited Versions of MacDonald's Sermons

Rolland Hein (ed): *Life Essential, The Hope of the Gospel* (Harold Shaw Publishers: Wheaton, Illinois, 1974).

Rolland Hein (ed): *George MacDonald, The Miracles of Our Lord* (Harold Shaw Publishers: Wheaton, Illinois, 1980).

Rolland Hein (ed): *Creation in Christ, Unspoken Sermons* (Harold Shaw Publishers: Wheaton, Illinois, 1976).

Edited Versions of MacDonald's Novels

Michael Phillips has edited more than twelve of the novels, published under different titles by Bethany House Publishers, Minneapolis.

More than a dozen versions of the novels, edited by Dan Hamilton and Elizabeth Hamilton, have been published by Victor Books, a Division of Scripture Press Publications: USA, Canada, England.

GEORGE MACDONALD

Part II: *Selections from his Writings*

(1) *The Holy Character of Our God*

THE DEEPEST IN GOD

NOW what is the deepest in *God?* His power? No, for power could not make him what we mean when we say *God.* Evil could, of course, never create one atom; but let us understand very plainly, that a being whose essence was only power would be such a negation of the divine that no righteous worship could be offered him: his service must be fear, and fear only. Such a being, even were he righteous in judgment, yet could not be God. The God himself whom we love could not be righteous were he not something deeper and better still than we generally mean by the word – but, alas, how little can language say without seeming to say something wrong! In one word, God is Love. Love is the deepest depth, the essence of his nature, at the root of all his being. It is not merely that he could not be God, if he had made no creatures to whom to be God; but love is the heart and hand of his creation; it is his right to create, and his power to create as well. The love that foresees creation is itself the power to create. Neither could he be righteous – that is, fair to his creatures – but that his love created them. His perfection is his love. All his divine rights rest upon his love. Ah, he is not the great monarch! The simplest peasant loving his cow, is more divine than any monarch whose monarchy is his glory. If God would not punish sin, or if he did it for anything but love, he would not be the father of Jesus Christ, the God who works as Jesus wrought.

What then, I say once more, is in Christ correspondent to the creative power of God? It must be something that comes also of love; and in the Son the love must be to the already existent. Because of that eternal love which has no beginning, the Father must have the Son. God could not love, could not be love, without making things to love: Jesus has God to love; the love of the Son is responsive to the love of the Father. The response to self-existent love is self-abnegating love. The refusal of himself is that in Jesus which corresponds to the creation of God. His love takes action, creates, in self-abjuration, in the death of self as motive; in the drowning of self in the life of God, where it lives only as love. What is life in a child? Is it not perfect response to his parents? Thorough oneness with them? A child at strife with his parents, one in whom their will is not his, is no child; as a child he is dead, and his death is manifest in rigidity and contortion. His spiritual order is on the way to chaos. Disintegration has begun. Death is at work in him. See the same child yielding to the will that is righteously above his own; see the life begin to flow from the heart through the members; see the relaxing limbs; see the light rise like a fountain in his eyes, and flash from his face! Life has again its lordship![1]

THE ETERNAL FATHERHOOD

Think, brothers, think, sisters, we walk in the air of an eternal fatherhood. Every uplifting of the heart is a looking up to The Father. Graciousness and truth around, above, beneath us, yea, *in* us. When we are least worthy, then, most tempted, hardest, unkindest let us yet commend our spirits into his hands. Whither else dare we send them? How the earthly father would love a child who would creep into his room with angry, troubled face, and sit down at his feet, saying when asked what he wanted: 'I feel so naughty, papa, I want to get good!' Would he say to his child: 'How dare you! Go away, and be good, and then come to me.' And shall we dare to think God would send us away if we came thus, and would not be pleased we came, even if we were angry as Jonah? Would we let all the tenderness of our nature flow forth upon such a child? And shall we dare to think that if we being evil know how to give good gifts to our children, God will not give us his own spirit when we come to ask him? Will not some heavenly dew descend cool upon the hot anger? some genial rain-drop on the dry selfishness? Some glance of sunlight on the cloudy hopelessness? Bread, at least, will be given, and not a stone; water, at least, will be sure, and not vinegar mingled with gall.

Nor is there anything we can ask for ourselves that we may not ask for another. We may commend any brother, any sister, to the common fatherhood. And there will be moments when, filled with that spirit which is the Lord, nothing will ease our hearts of their love but the commending of all men, all our brothers, all our sisters, to the one Father. Nor shall we ever know that repose in the Father's hands, that rest of the Holy Sepulchre, which the Lord knew when the agony of death was over, when the storm of the world died away behind his retiring spirit, and he entered the regions where there is only life, and therefore all that is not music is silence, (for all noise comes of the conflict of Life and Death) – we shall never be able, I say, to rest in the bosom of the Father, till the fatherhood is fully revealed to us in the love of the brothers. For he cannot be our father save as he is their father; and if we do not see him and feel him as their father, we cannot know him as ours. Never shall we know him aright until we rejoice and exult for our race that he is *the* Father. He that loveth not his brother whom he hath seen, how can he love God whom he hath not seen? To rest, I say, at last, even in those hands into which the Lord commended his spirit, we must have learned already *to love our neighbour as ourselves.*[2]

THE CHILD-LIKE HUMILITY
OF GOD IN CHRIST

But to advance now to the highest point of this teaching of our Lord: 'He that receiveth me receiveth him that sent me.' To receive a child in the name of God is to receive God himself. How to receive him? As alone he can be received – by knowing him as he is. To know him is to have him in us. And that we may know him, let us now receive this revelation of him, in the words of our Lord himself. Here is the argument of highest import founded upon the teaching of our master in the utterance before us. God is represented in Jesus, for that God is like Jesus: Jesus is represented in the child, for that

Jesus is like the child. Therefore God is represented in the child, for that he is like the child. God is child-like. In the true vision of this fact lies the receiving of God in the child.

Having reached this point, I have nothing more to do with the argument; for if the Lord meant this – that is if this be a truth, he that is able to receive it will receive it: he that hath ears to hear it will hear it. For our Lord's arguments are for the presentation of the truth and the truth carries its own conviction to him who is able to receive it.

But the word of one who has seen this truth may help the dawn of a like perception in those who keep their faces turned towards the east and its aurora; for men may have eyes, and, seeing dimly, want to see more. Therefore let us brood a little over the idea itself, and see whether it will not come forth so as to commend itself to that spirit, which, one with the human spirit where it dwells, searches the deep things of God. For, although the true heart may at first be shocked at the truth, as Peter was shocked when he said, 'That be far from thee, Lord', yet will it, after a season, receive it and rejoice in in it.

Let me then ask, Do you believe in the Incarnation? And if you do, let me ask further, Was Jesus ever less divine than God? I answer for you, Never. He was lower, but never less divine. Was he not a child then? You answer, Yes, but not like other children. I ask, Did he not look like other children? If he looked like them and was not like them, the whole was a deception, a masquerade at best. I say he was a child, whatever more he might be. God is man, and infinitely more. Our Lord became flesh, but did not *become* man. He took on him the form of man: he was man already. And he was, is, and ever shall be divinely child-like. He could never have been a child if he would ever have ceased to be a child, for in him the transient found nothing. Childhood belongs to the divine nature. Obedience then is as divine as Will, Service as divine as Rule. How? Because they are one in their nature; they are both a doing of the truth.

The love in them is the same. The Fatherhood and the Sonship are one, save that the Fatherhood looks down lovingly, and the Sonship looks up lovingly. Love is all. And God is all in all. He is ever seeking to get down to us – to be the divine man to us. And we are ever saying, That be far from thee, Lord! We are careful, in our unbelief, over the divine dignity, of which he is too grand to think. Better pleasing to God, it needs little daring to say, is the audacity of Job, who, rushing into his presence, and flinging the door of his presence-chamber to the wall, like a troubled, it may be angry, but yet faithful child, calls aloud in the ear of him whose perfect Father-hood he has yet to learn: 'Am I a sea or a whale, that thou settest a watch over me?'

Let us dare, then, to climb the height of divine truth to which this utterance of our Lord would lead us. Does it not lead us up hither: that the devotion of God to his creatures is perfect? that he does not think about himself but about them? that he wants nothing for himself, but finds his blessedness in the outgoing of blessedness?

Ah! it is a terrible – shall it be a lonely glory this? We will draw near with our human response, our abandonment of self in the faith of Jesus. He gives himself to us – shall not we give ourselves to him? Shall we not give ourselves to each other whom he loves? For when is the child the ideal child in our eyes and to our hearts? Is it not when with gentle hand he takes his father by the beard, and turns that father's face up to his brothers and sisters to kiss? when even the lovely selfishness of love-seeking has vanished, and the heart is absorbed in loving?

In this, then, is God like the child: that he is simply and altogether our friend, our father – our more than friend, father, and mother – our infinite love-perfect God. Grand and strong beyond all that human imagination can conceive of poet-thinking and kingly action, he is delicate beyond all that human tenderness can conceive of husband or wife, homely beyond all that human heart can conceive of father or mother. He has not two thoughts about us. With him all is simplicity of purpose and meaning and effort and end – namely, that we should be as he is, think the same thoughts, mean the same things, possess the same blessedness. It is so plain that any one may see it, every one ought to see it, every one shall see it. It must be so. He is utterly true and good to us, nor shall anything withstand his will.[3]

Our Home in God

How terribly, then, have the theologians misrepresented God in the measures of the low and showy, not the lofty and simple humanities! Nearly all of them represent him as a great King on a grand throne, thinking how grand he is, and making it the business of his being and the end of his universe to keep up his glory, wielding the bolts of a Jupiter against them that take his name in vain. They would not allow this, but follow out what they say, and it comes much to this.

Brothers, have you found our king? There he is, kissing little children and saying they are like God. There he is at table with the head of a fisherman lying on his bosom, and somewhat heavy at heart that even he, the beloved disciple, cannot yet understand him well. The simplest peasant who loves his children and his sheep were – no, not a truer, for the other is false, but – a true type of our God beside that monstrosity of a monarch.

The God who is ever uttering himself in the changeful profusions of nature; who takes millions of years to form a soul that shall understand him and be blessed; who never needs to be, and never is, in haste; who welcomes the simplest thought of truth or beauty as the return for seed he has sown upon the old fallows of eternity; who rejoices in the response a faltering moment to the age-long cry of his wisdom in the streets; the God of music, of painting, of building, the Lord of Hosts, the God of mountains and oceans; whose laws go forth from one unseen point of wisdom, and thither return without an atom of loss; the God of history working in time unto Christianity; this God is the God of little children, and he alone can be perfectly, abandonedly simple and devoted. The deepest, purest love of a woman has its well-spring in him. Our longing desires can no more exhaust the fulness of the treasures of the God-head, than our imagination can touch their measure. Of him not a thought, not a joy, not a hope of one of his creatures can pass unseen; and while one of them remains unsatisfied, he is not Lord over all.

Therefore, with angels and with archangels, with the spirits of the just made perfect, with the little children of the kingdom, yea, with the Lord himself, and for all them that know him not, we praise and magnify and laud his name in itself, saying *Our Father*. We do not draw back for that we are unworthy, nor even for that we are hard-hearted and care not for the good. For it is his childlikeness that makes him our God and Father. The perfection of his relation to us swallows up all our imperfections, all our defects, all our evils; for our childhood is born of his fatherhood. That man is perfect in faith who can come to God in the utter dearth of his feelings and his desires, without a glow or an aspiration, with the weight of low thoughts, failures, neglects, and wandering forgetfulness, and say to him, 'Thou art my refuge, because thou art my home'.

Such a faith will not lead to presumption. The man who can pray such a prayer will know better than another that God is not mocked; that he is not a man that he should repent; that tears and entreaties will not work on him to the breach of one of his laws; that for God to give a man because he asked for it that which was not in harmony with his laws of truth and right, would be to damn him – to cast him into the outer darkness. And he knows that out of that prison the childlike, imperturbable God will let no man come till he has paid the uttermost farthing.

And if he should forget this, the God to whom he belongs does not forget it, does not forget him. Life is no series of chances with a few providences sprinkled between to keep up a justly failing belief, but one providence of God; and the man shall not live long before life itself shall remind him, it may be in agony of soul, of that which he has forgotten. When he prays for comfort, the answer may come in dismay and terror and the turning aside of the Father's countenance; for love itself will, for love's sake, turn the countenance away from that which is not lovely; and he will have to read, written upon the dark wall of his imprisoned conscience, the words, awful and glorious, *Our God is a consuming fire.*[4]

GOD'S HOLY LOVE

Commenting on Hebrews 12: 29 – *Our God is a consuming fire.*

Nothing is inexorable but love. Love which will yield to prayer is imperfect and poor. Nor is it then the love that yields, but its alloy .... For love loves unto purity. Love has ever in view the absolute loveliness of that which it beholds. Where loveliness is incomplete, and love cannot love its fill of loving, it spends itself to make more lovely, that it may love more; it strives for perfection, even that itself may be perfected – not in itself; but in the object .... Therefore, all that is not beautiful in the beloved, all that comes between and is not of love's kind, must be destroyed. And our God is a consuming fire.[5]

GOD'S CREATIVE AND RECREATING LOVE

'I do not believe that *mere* punishment exists anywhere in the economy of the highest; I think *mere* punishment a human idea, not a divine one. But the consuming fire is more terrible than any punishment invented by riotous and cruel imagination. Punishment indeed it is – not *mere* punishment; a power of God for his creature. Love is God's being; love is his creative energy; they are one: God's punishments are for the casting out of the sin that uncreates, for the recreating of the things his love made and sin has unmade.'[6]

CALLING ON GOD

'Oh, if he were called anything else than Father! I am afraid I hate my father.'

'I don't wonder. But that is your own fault, too.'

'How is that, sir? Surely you are making even me out worse than I am.'

'No. You are afraid of him. As soon as you have ceased to be afraid of him, you will no longer be in danger of hating him.'

'I can't help being afraid of him.'

'You must break the bonds of that slavery. No slave can be God's servant. His servants are all free men. But we will come to that presently. You must not try to call God your Father, till father means something very different to you from what it seems to mean now. Think of the grandest human being you can imagine – the tenderest, the most gracious, whose severity is boundless, but thrusts himself most – all against evil, all for the evil-doer. God is all that, and infinitely more. You need not call him by any name till that name bursts from your heart. God our Saviour means all the names in the world, and infinitely more! One thing I can assure you of, that even I, if you will but do your duty in regard to this thing, will not only love – yes, I will say that word – will not only love, but honour you far more than if I had known you only as a respectable youth. It is harder to turn back than to keep at home. I doubt if there could be such joy in heaven over the repenting sinner if he was never to be free of his disgrace. But I like you the better for having the feeling of eternal disgrace now.'[7]

SO RICH A LOVE

Once, expressing to Margaret her regret that she should be so much a trouble to her, she said: 'You have to do so much for me, that I am ashamed.'

'Do let me wash the feet of one of his disciples,' Margaret replied, gently expostulating; after which, Euphra never grumbled at her own demands upon her.

Again, one day, she said: 'I am not right at all to-day, Margaret. God can't love me, I'm so hateful.'

'Don't measure God's mind by your own, Euphra. It would be a poor love that depended not on itself, but on the feelings of the person loved. A crying baby turns away from its mother's breast, but she does not put it away till it stops crying. She holds it closer. For my part, in the worst mood I am ever in, when I don't feel I love God at all, I just look up to his love, and say to him: "Look at me. See what state I am in. Help me!" Ah! you would wonder how that makes peace. And the love comes of itself; sometimes so strong, it nearly breaks my heart.'

'But there is a text I don't like.'

'Take another, then.'

'But it will keep coming.'

'Give it back to God, and never mind it.'

'But would that be right?'

'One day, when I was a little girl, so high, I couldn't eat my porridge and sat looking at it. "Eat your porridge," said my mother. "I don't want it," I answered. "There's nothing else for you," said my mother – for she had not learned so much from my father then, as she did before he died. "Hoots!" said my father – I cannot, dear Euphra, make *his* words into English.'

'No, no don't,' said Euphra; 'I shall understand them perfectly.'

'"Hoots! Janet, my woman!" said my father. "Gie the bairn a dish o' tay. Wadna ye like some tay, Maggy, my doo?" "Ay wad I," said I. "The parritch is guid eneuch," said my mother. "Nae doot aboot the parritch, woman; it's the bairn's stamack, it's no the parritch." My mother said no more, but made me a cup of such nice tea; for whenever she gave in, she gave in quite. I drank it; and, half from anxiety to please my mother, half from reviving hunger, attacked the porridge next, and ate it up. "Leuk at that!" said my father. "Janet, my woman, gie a body the guid they can tak', an' they'll sune tak' the guid that they canna. Ye're better noo, Maggy, my doo?" I never told him that I had taken the porridge too soon after all, and had to creep into the wood, and be sick. But it is all the same for the story.'[8]

(2) *The Life and Ministry of Jesus Our Brother*

FATHER AND SON: GOD OUR SAVIOUR

I would help some to understand what Jesus came from the home of our Father to be to us and do for us. Everything in the world is more or less misunderstood at first: we have to learn what it is, and come at length to see that it must be so, that it could not be otherwise. Then we know it; and we never know a thing *really* until we know it thus. I presume there is scarce a human being who, resolved to speak openly, would not confess to having something that plagued him, something from which he would gladly be free, something rendering it impossible for him, at the moment, to regard life as an altogether good thing ....

However absurd the statement may appear to one who has not yet discovered the fact for himself, the cause of every man's discomfort is evil, moral evil – first of all, evil in himself, his own sin, his own wrongness, his own unrightness; and then, evil in those he loves: with this latter I have not now to deal; the only way to get rid of it, is for the man to get rid of his own sin. No special sin may be recognizable as having caused this or that special physical discomfort – which may indeed have originated with some ancestor; but evil in ourselves is the cause of its continuance, the source of its necessity, and the preventive of that patience which would soon take from it, or at least blunt its sting. The evil is *essentially* unnecessary, and passes with the attainment of the object for which it is permitted, namely the development of pure will in man; the suffering also is essentially unnecessary, but while the evil lasts, the suffering, whether consequent or merely concomitant, is absolutely necessary. Foolish is the man, and there are many such men, who would rid himself or his fellows of discomfort by setting the world right, by waging war on the evils around him, while he neglects that integral part of the world where lies his business, his first business – namely, his own character and conduct. Were it possible – an absurd supposition – that the world should thus be righted from the outside, it would yet be impossible for the man who had contributed to the work, remaining what he was, ever to enjoy the perfection of the result; himself not in tune with the organ he had tuned, he must imagine it still a distracted, jarring instrument .... There is no way of making three men right but by making right each one of the three; but a cure in one man who repents and turns, is a beginning of the cure of the whole human race.

Even if a man's suffering be a far inheritance, for the curing of which by faith and obedience this life would not be sufficiently long, faith and obedience will yet render it endurable to the man, and overflow in help to his fellow-sufferers. The groaning body, wrapt in the garment of hope, will, with outstretched neck, look for its redemption, and endure.

The one cure for any organism, is to be set right – to have all its parts brought into harmony with each other; the one comfort is to know this cure in process. Rightness alone is cure. The return of the organism to its true self, is its only possible ease. To free a man from suffering, he must be set right, put in health; and the health at the root of man's being, his rightness, is to be free from wrongness, that is, from sin. A man is right when there is no wrong in him. The wrong, the evil is in him; he must be set free from it. I do not mean set free from the sins he has done: that will follow; I mean the sins he is doing, or is capable of doing; the sins in his being which spoil his nature – the wrongness in him – the evil he consents to; the sin he is, which makes him do the sin he does.

To save a man from his sins, is to say to him, in [a] sense perfect and eternal, 'Rise up and walk. Be at liberty in thy essential being. Be free as the son of God is free'. To do this for us, Jesus was born, and remains born to all the ages. When misery drives a man to call out to the source of his life, – and I take the increasing outcry against existence as a sign of the growth of the race toward a sense of the need of regeneration – the answer, I think, will come in a quickening of his conscience. This earnest of the promised deliverance may not, in all probability will not be what the man desires; he will want only to be rid of his suffering; but that he cannot have, save in being delivered from its essential root, a thing infinitely worse than any suffering it can produce. If he will not have that deliverance he must keep his suffering. Through chastisement he will take at last the only way that leads into the liberty of that which is and must be. There can be no deliverance but to come out of his evil dream into the glory of God.

It is true that Jesus came, in delivering us from our sins, to deliver us also from the painful consequences of our sins. But these consequences exist by the one law of the universe, the true will of the Perfect. That broken, that disobeyed by the creature, disorganization renders suffering inevitable; it is the natural consequence of the unnatural – and, in the perfection of God's creation, the result is curative of the cause; the pain at least tends to the healing of the breach. The Lord never came to deliver men from the consequences of their sins while yet those sins remained: that would be to cast out of window the medicine of cure while yet the man lay sick; to go dead against the very laws of being. Yet men, loving their sins, and feeling nothing of their dread hatefulness, have, consistently with their low condition, constantly taken this word concerning the Lord to mean that he came to save them from the punishment of their sins. The idea – the miserable fancy rather – has terribly corrupted the preaching of the gospel. The message of the good news has not been truly delivered. Unable to believe in the forgiveness of their Father in heaven, imagining him not at liberty to forgive, or incapable of forgiving forthright; not really believing him God our Saviour, but a God bound, either in his own nature or by a law above him and compulsory upon him, to exact some recompense or satisfaction for sin, a multitude of teaching men have taught their fellows that Jesus came to bear our punishment and save us from hell. They have represented a result as the object of his mission – the said result nowise to be desired by true man save as consequent on the gain of his object. The mission of Jesus was from the same source and with the same object as the punishment of our sins. He came to work along with our punishment. He came to side with it, and set us free from our sins. No man is safe from hell until he is free from his sins; but a man to whom his sins, that is the evil things in him, are a burden, while he may indeed sometimes feel as if he were in hell, will soon have forgotten that ever he had any other hell to think of than that of his sinful condition. For to him his sins are hell; he would go to the other hell to be free of them; free of them, hell itself would be endurable to him. For hell is God's and not the devil's. Hell is on the side of God and man, to free the child of God from the corruption of death. Not one soul will ever be redeemed from hell but by being saved from his sins, from the evil in him. If hell be needful to save him, hell will blaze, and the worm will writhe and bite, until he takes refuge in the will of the Father. 'Salvation from hell' is salvation as conceived by such to whom hell, and not evil, is the terror. But if even for dread of hell a poor soul seek the Father, he will be heard of him in his terror, and, taught of him to seek the immeasurably greater gift, will in the greater receive the less.[9]

The Nurturing of Our Faith

The story of the daughter of Jairus is recorded briefly by St Matthew, more fully by St Luke, most fully by St Mark [5:21-43]. One of the rulers of the synagogue at Capernaum falls at the feet of our Lord, saying his little daughter is at the point of death. She was about twelve years of age. He begs the Lord to lay his hands on her that she may live. Our Lord goes with him, followed by many people. On his way to restore the child he is arrested by a touch. He makes no haste to outstrip death. We can imagine the impatience of the father when the Lord stood and asked who touched him. What did that matter? His daughter was dying; Death would not wait. But the woman's heart and soul must not be passed by. The father with the only daughter must wait yet a little. The will of God cannot be outstripped.

'While he yet spake, there came from the ruler of the synagogue's house certain which said, "Thy daughter is dead: why troublest thou the Master any further?"'

'Ah! I thought so! There it is! Death has won the race!' we may suppose the father to say – bitterly within himself. But Jesus, while he tried the faith of men, never tried it without feeding its strength. With the trial he always gives the way of escape. 'As soon as Jesus heard the word that was spoken' – not leaving it to work its agony of despair first – 'he saith unto the ruler of the synagogue, "Be not afraid; only believe".'

They are such simple words – commonplace in the ears of those who have heard them often and heeded them little! but containing more for this man's peace than all the consolations of philosophy, than all the enforcements of morality; yea, even than the raising of his daughter itself. To arouse the higher, the hopeful, the trusting nature of a man; to cause him to look up into the unknown region of mysterious possibilities – the God so poorly known – is to do infinitely more for a man than to remove the pressure of the direst evil without it. I will go further: To arouse the hope that there may be a God with a heart like our own is more for the humanity in us than to produce the absolute conviction that there is a being who made the heaven and the earth and the sea and the fountains of waters. Jesus is the express image of God's substance, and in him we know the heart of God. To nourish faith in himself was the best thing he could do for the man. We hear of no word from the ruler further. If he answered not our Lord in words, it is no wonder. The compressed lip and the uplifted eye would say more than any words to the heart of the Saviour.[10]

BECOMING SONS LIKE HIMSELF
Reflections on John 8: 31-36.

But one who reads may call out, in the agony and thirst of a child waking from a dream of endless seeking and no finding, 'I am bound like Lazarus in his grave-clothes! what am I to do?' Here is the answer, drawn from this parable of our Lord; for the saying is much like a parable, teaching more than it utters, appealing to the conscience and heart, not to the understanding: [']You are a slave; the slave has no hold on the house; only the sons and daughters have an abiding rest in the home of their father. God cannot have slaves about him always. You must give up your slavery, and be set free from it. That is what I am here for. If I make you free, you shall be free indeed; for I can make you free only by making you what you were meant to be, sons like myself. That is how alone the Son can work. But it is you who must become sons; you must will it, and I am here to help you.' It is as if he said, 'You shall have the freedom of my father's universe; for, free from yourselves, you will be free of his heart. Yourselves are your slavery. That is the darkness which you have loved rather than the light. You have given honour to yourselves, and not to the Father; you have sought honour from men, and not from the Father! Therefore, even in the house of your father, you have been but sojourning slaves. We in his family are all one; we have no party-spirit; we have no self-seeking: fall in with us, and you shall be free as we are free.'

If then the poor starved child cry – 'How, Lord?' the answer will depend on what he means by that *how*. If he means, 'What plan wilt thou adopt? What is thy scheme for cutting my bonds and setting me free?' the answer may be a deepening of the darkness, a tightening of the bonds. But if he means, 'Lord, what wouldst thou have me to do?' the answer will not tarry. 'Give yourself to me to do what I tell you, to understand what I say, to be my good, obedient little brother, and I will wake in you the heart that my father put in you, the same kind of heart that I have, and it will grow to love the Father, altogether and absolutely, as mine does, till you are ready to be torn to pieces for him. Then you will know that you are at the heart of the universe, at the heart of every secret – at the heart of the Father. Not till then will you be free, then free indeed!'

Christ died to save us, not from suffering, but from ourselves; not from injustice, far less from justice, but from being unjust. He died that we might live – but live as he lives, by dying as he died who died to himself that he might live unto God. If we do not die to ourselves, we cannot live to God, and he that does not live to God, is dead. 'Ye shall know the truth,' the Lord says, 'and the truth shall make you free. I am the truth, and you shall be free as I am free. To be free, you must be sons like me. To be free you must be that which you have to be, that which you are created. To be free you must give the answer of sons to the Father who calls you. To be free you must fear nothing but evil, care for nothing but the will of the Father, hold to him in absolute confidence and infinite expectation. He alone is to be trusted.' He has shown us the Father not only by doing what the Father does, not only by loving his Father's children even as the Father loves them, but by his perfect satisfaction with him, his joy in him, his utter obedience to him, He has shown us the Father by the absolute devotion of a perfect son. He is the Son of God because the Father and he are one, have one thought, one mind, one heart. Upon this truth – I do not mean the dogma, but the truth itself of Jesus to his father – hangs the universe; and upon the recognition of this truth – that is, upon their becoming thus true – hangs the freedom of the children, the redemption of their whole world. 'I and the Father are one,' is the centre-truth of the Universe; and the circumfering truth is, 'that they also may be one in us.'

The only free man, then, is he who is a child the Father. He is a servant of all, but can be made the slave of none: he is a son of the lord of the universe. He is in himself, in virtue of his truth, free. He is in himself a king. For the Son rests his claim to royalty on this, that *he was born and came into the world to bear witness to the truth.* [11]

JESUS' MINISTRY AMONG THE SUFFERING
Speaking of the death of Lazarus as recorded in
the Gospel of John, chapter 11.

But oh, my friends, what shall I say about this wonderful message? Think of being sick for the glory of God! of being shipwrecked for the glory of God! of being drowned for the glory of God! How can the sickness, the fear, the brokenheartedness of his creatures be for the glory of God? What kind of a God can that be? Why just a God so perfectly, absolutely good that the things that look least like it are only the means of clearing our eyes to let us see how good he is. For he is so good that he is not satisfied with being good. He loves his children so, that except he can make them good like himself, make them blessed by seeing how good he is, and desiring the same goodness in themselves, he is not satisfied. He is not like a fine, proud benefactor, who is content with doing that which will satisfy his sense of his own glory, but like a mother who puts her arm round her child, and whose heart is sore till she can make her child see the love which is her glory. The glorification of the Son of God is the glorification of the human race, for the glory of God is the glory of man, and that glory is love! Welcome sickness, welcome sorrow, welcome death, revealing that glory! [12]

HEALING LOVE
A minister takes home a vagrant
young woman who has lost her illegitimate infant.

'Oh, sir, but ye are good to me!' she resumed. ' That brae just minded me o' the Hill of Difficulty in the *Pilgrim's Progress.*'

'You know that story, then?' said the minister.

'My old grannie used to make me read it to her as she lay dying. I thought it long and tiresome then, but since you took me home, I have remembered many things in it: I had come to the house of the Interpreter. You've made me understand, sir!'

'I am glad of that, Isy! You see I know some things that make me very glad, and I want them to make you glad too. And the thing that makes me gladdest of all is just that God is what he is. To know that such a being is God over us and in us, makes our very existence a most precious delight. His children, those of them that know him, are all glad just because he is and they are his children. Do you think a strong man like me would read sermons and say prayers and talk to people, and do nothing but such shamefully easy work, if he did not believe what he said?'

'I'm sure, sir, you had hard enough work with me! I am a bad one to teach! I thought I knew all that you have had such trouble to make me see! I was in a bog of ignorance and misery, but now I am getting my head up, and seeing about me! Please, let me ask you one thing, sir – how is it that, when the thought of God comes to me, I always draw back, afraid of him? If he be the kind of person you say he is, why can't I go close up to him?'

'I confess to the same foolishness at times,' answered the minister. 'It can only be because we do not yet see God as he is – and that must be because we do not yet really understand Jesus – do not see the glory of God in his face. God is just like him.'

And the parson fell awondering why it could be that so many, gentle and guileless as this woman-child, should recoil from the thought of the perfect One. Why should they not be always and irresistibly drawn toward the very idea of God? Why should they not run to see and make sure whether God were indeed such a one or not? whether he was really Love itself, or only after a fashion? It made him think about many things – concerning which he soon discovered that he had been teaching them without knowing them – for, indeed, how could he know things that were not true and therefore could not be known? He had indeed been saying that God was Love, and yet teaching many things about him that were not lovable! They sat thinking and talking, with silence between; and, all the time, the day-star was rising unnoted in their hearts. At length they rose themselves and resumed their journey.

The door stood open to receive them, but ere they reached it a bright-looking little woman, with delicate lines of ingrained red in a sorrowful, waiting face, appeared in it, looking out for them with questioning eyes, like a mother-bird whose feet were just leaving hold of the threshold of her nest to fly to meet them. Through the film that blinded her expectant eyes, Marion saw at once what manner of woman she was who drew nigh, and her motherhood went out to welcome her. In the love-witchery of the yearning look that humbly sought acceptance, in the hesitating approach, half-checked by gentle apology, Marion seemed to see her own Isy returned from the gates of Death, and sprang to meet her. The mediating love of the minister, obliterating itself, had made him draw lingering back a step or two, and wait for what would follow; but when he saw the two folded each in the other's arms, and the fountain of eternal love break forth at once from the two encountering hearts, his soul leaped for joy at the birth of a new love, new indeed, but not the less surely eternal, for God is Love, and Love is that which is, and was, and shall be for evermore, boundless, unconditioned, self-existent, creative!

'Truly,' he said in himself, 'God is Love, and God is all and in all! He is no abstraction, but the one eternal Individual! In him Love evermore breaks forth anew into fresh personality in every new consciousness, in every new child of the one creating Father. In every burning heart, in every thing that hopes and fears and is, Love is the creative presence, the centre, the source of life, yea, Life itself; yea, God himself!'[13]

(3) *The Glorious Love of Father and Son in the Spirit*

The Self-giving of the Son to the Father

Let us not forget that the devotion of the Son could never have been but for the devotion of the Father, who never seeks his own glory one atom more than does the Son; who is devoted to the Son, and to all his sons and daughters, with a devotion perfect and eternal, with fathomless unselfishness. The whole being and doing of Jesus on earth is the same as his being and doing from all eternity, that whereby he is the blessed son-God of the father-God; it is the shining out of that life that men might see it. It is a being like God, a doing of the will of God, a working of the works of God, therefore an unveiling of the Father in the Son, that men may know him. It is the prayer of the Son to the rest of the sons to come back to the Father, to be reconciled to the Father, to behave to the Father as he does. He seems to me to say: 'I know your father, for he is my father; I know him because I have been with him from eternity. You do not know him; I have come to you to tell you that as I am, such is he; that he is just like me, only greater and better. He only is the true, original good; I am true because I seek nothing but his will. He only is all in all; I am not all in all, but he is my father, and I am the son in whom his heart of love is satisfied. Come home with me, and sit with me on the throne of my obedience. Together we will do his will, and be glad with him, for his will is the only good. You may do with me as you please; I will not defend myself. Because I speak true, my witness is unswerving; I stand to it, come what may. If I held my face to my testimony only till danger came close, and then prayed the Father for twelve legions of angels to deliver me, that would be to say the Father would do anything for his children until it began to hurt him. I bear witness that my father is such as I. In the face of death I assert it, and dare death to disprove it. Kill me; do what you will and can against me; my father is true, and I am true in saying that he is true. Danger or hurt cannot turn me aside from this my witness. Death can only kill my body; he cannot make me his captive. Father, thy will be done! The pain will pass; it will be but for a time! Gladly will I suffer that men may know that I live, and that thou art my life. Be with me, father, that it may not be more than I can bear.'[14]

The Mutual Joy
of the Son in the Father
and the Father in the Son

In a discussion with a youth (Matthew 19: 16ff), Jesus raises the
question as to why the young man calls him 'good'. Jesus comments:
'There is none good save one, even God.' Following this cue,
MacDonald expands on Jesus' relationship with his good heavenly
Father and the unique and reserved place it takes.

The words with which the Lord interrupts his address reveal the
whole attitude of the Lord's being. At that moment, at every and
each moment, just as much as when in the garden of Gethsemane,
or encountering any of those hours which men call crises of life, his
whole thought, his whole delight, was in the thought, in the will,
in the being of his Father. The joy of the Lord's life, that which
made it life to him, was the Father; of him he was always thinking,
to him he was always turning.

I suppose most men have some thought of pleasure or satisfaction
or strength to which they turn when action pauses, life becomes
for a moment still, and the wheel sleeps on its own swiftness: with
Jesus it needed no pause of action, no rush of renewed consciousness,
to send him home; his thought was ever and always his Father. To
its home in the heart of the Father his heart ever turned. That was
his treasure-house, the jewel of his mind, the mystery of his gladness,
claiming all degrees and shades of delight, from peace and calmest
content to ecstasy. His life was hid in God. No vain show could
enter at his eyes; every truth and grandeur of life passed before him
as it was; neither ambition nor disappointment could distort them
to his eternal childlike gaze; he beheld and loved them from the
bosom of the Father. It was not for himself he came to the world –
– not to establish his own power over the doings, his own influence
over the hearts of men: he came that they might know the Father
who was his joy, his life. The sons of men were his Father's children
like himself: that he should have them all in his bosom was the one
thought of his heart: that should be his doing for his Father, cost him
what it might! He came to do his will, and on the earth was the same

he had from the beginning, the eternal first. He was not interested in himself, but in his Father and in his Father's children. He did not care to hear himself called good. It was not of consequence to him. He was there to let men see the goodness of the Father in whom he gloried. For that he entered the weary dream of the world, which the glory was so dulled and clouded. 'You call *me* good! You should know my Father!' For the Lord's greatness consisted in his Father being greater than he: who calls into being is greater than who is called. The Father was always the Father, the Son always the Son; yet the Son not of himself, but by the Father; he does not live by his own power, like the Father. If there were no Father, there would be no Son. All that is the Lord's is the Father's, and all that is the Father's he has given to the Son. The Lord's goodness is of the Father's goodness; because the Father is good the Son is good. When the word *good* enters the ears of the Son, his heart lifts it at once to his Father, the Father of all. His words contain no denial of goodness in himself: in his grand self-regard he was not the original of his goodness, neither did he care for his own goodness, except to be good: it was to him a matter of course. But for his Father's goodness, he would spend life, suffering, labour, death, to make that known! His other children must learn to give Him his due, and love him as did the primal Son! The Father was all in all to the Son, and the Son no more thought of his own goodness than an honest man thinks of his honesty. When the good man sees goodness, he thinks of his own evil: Jesus had no evil to think of, but neither does he think of his goodness; he delights in his Father's. 'Why callest thou me good? None is good save one, even God.'[15]

FATHER AND SON AT WORK TOGETHER

Man finds it hard to get what he wants, because he does not want the best; God finds it hard to give, because he would give the best, and man will not take it. What Jesus did, was what the Father is always doing; the suffering he endured was that of the Father from the foundation of the world, reaching its climax in the person of his Son. God provides the sacrifice; the sacrifice is himself. He is always, and has ever been, sacrificing himself to and for his creatures. It lies in the very essence of his creation of them. The worst heresy, next to that of dividing religion and righteousness, is to divide the Father from the Son – in thought or feeling or action or intent; to represent the Son as doing that which the Father does not himself do. Jesus did nothing but what the Father did and does. If Jesus suffered for men, it was because his Father suffers for men; only he came close to men through his body and their senses, that he might bring their spirits close to his Father and their Father, so giving them life, and losing what could be lost of his own. He is God our Saviour: it is because God is our Saviour that Jesus is our Saviour. The God and Father of Jesus Christ could never possibly be satisfied with less than giving himself to his own!

The unbeliever may easily imagine a better God than the common theology of the country offers him; but not the lovingest heart that ever beat can even reflect the length and breadth and depth and height of that love of God which shows itself in his Son – one, and of one mind, with himself. The whole history is a divine agony to give divine life to creatures. The outcome of that agony, the victory of that creative and again creative energy, will be radiant life, whereof joy unspeakable is the flower. Every child will look in the eyes of the Father; and the eyes of the Father will receive the child with an infinite embrace.[16]

THE BOND OF THE UNIVERSE

Friends, if you think anything less than this could redeem the world, or make blessed any child that God has created, you know neither the Son nor the Father.

The bond of the universe, the chain that holds it together, the one active unity, the harmony of things, the negation of difference, the reconciliation of all forms, all shows, all wandering desires, all returning loves; the fact at the root of every vision; revealing that 'love is the only good in the world', and selfishness the one thing hateful, in the city of the living God unutterable, is the devotion of the Son to the Father. It is the life of the universe. It is not the fact that

God created all things, that makes the universe a whole; but that he through whom he created them loves him perfectly, is eternally content in his father, is satisfied to be because his father is with him. It is not the fact that God is all in all, that unites the universe; it is the love of the Son to the Father. For of no onehood comes unity; there can be no oneness where there is only one. For the very beginnings of unity there must be two. Without Christ, therefore, there could be no universe. The reconciliation wrought by Jesus is not the primary source of unity, of safety to the world; that reconciliation was the necessary working out of the eternal antecedent fact, the fact making itself potent upon the rest of the family – that God and Christ are one, are father and son, the Father loving the Son as only the Father can love, the Son loving the Father as only the Son can love. The prayer of the Lord for unity between men and the Father and himself, springs from the eternal need of love. The more I regard it, the more I am lost in the wonder and glory of the thing. But for the Father and the Son, no two would care a jot the one for the other. It might be the right way for creatures to love because of mere existence, but what two creatures would ever have originated the loving? I cannot for a moment believe it would have been I. Even had I come into being as now with an inclination to love, selfishness would soon have overborne it. But if the Father loves the Son, if the very music that makes the harmony of life lies, not in the theory of love in the heart of the Father, but in the fact of it, in the burning love in the hearts of Father and Son, and to the spirit of both, the fatherhood of the Father meeting and blending with the sonhood of the Son, and drawing us up into the glory of their joy, to share in the thoughts of love that pass between them, in their thoughts of delight and rest in each other, in their thoughts of joy in all the little ones. The life of Jesus is the light of men, revealing to them the Father.[17]

THE SHARED SUFFERINGS OF JESUS CHRIST

'My lady!' he repeated, just a little embarrassed, 'I should like to tell you one thing that came to me only lately – came to me when thinking over the hard words you spoke to me that day in the park. But it is something so awful that I dare not speak of it except you will make your heart solemn to hear it.'

He stopped, with his eyes questioning hers. Clementina's first thought once more was madness, but as she steadily returned his look, her face grew pale, and she gently bowed her head in consent.

'I will try then,' said Malcolm. 'Everybody knows what few think about, that once there lived a man who, in the broad face of prejudiced respectability, truth-hating hypocrisy, common place religion, and dull book-learning, affirmed that he knew the secret of life, and understood the heart and history of men – who wept over their sorrows, yet worshipped the God of the whole earth, saying that he had known him from eternal days. The same said that he came to do what the Father did, and that he did nothing but what he had learned of the Father. They killed him, you know, my lady, in a terrible way that one is afraid even to think of. But he insisted that he laid down his life; that he allowed them to take it. Now I ask whether that grandest thing, crowning his life, the yielding of it to the hand of violence, he had not learned also from his Father. Was his death the only thing he had not so learned? If I am right, and I do not say if in doubt, then the suffering of those three terrible hours was a type of the suffering of the Father himself in bringing sons and daughters through the cleansing and glorifying fires without which the created cannot be made the very children of God, partakers of the divine nature and peace. Then from the lowest, weakest tone of suffering, up to the loftiest pitch, the divinest acme of pain, there is not one pang to which the sensorium of the universe does not respond; never an untuneful vibration of nerve or spirit but thrills beyond the brain or the heart of the sufferer to the brain, the heart of the universe; and God, in the simplest, most literal, fullest sense, and not by sympathy alone, suffers with his creatures.'

'Well, but he is able to bear it; they are not: I cannot bring myself to see the right of it.'

'Nor will you, my lady, so long as you cannot bring yourself to see the good they get by it – My lady, when I was trying my best with poor Kelpie, you would not listen to me.'

'You are ungenerous,' said Clementina, flushing.

'My lady,' persisted Malcolm, 'you would not understand me. You denied me a heart because of what seemed in your eyes cruelty. I knew that I was saving her from death at the least, probably from a life of torture: God may be good, though to you his government may seem to deny it. There is but one way God cares to govern – the way of the Father-king – and that way is at hand – But I have yet given you only the one half of my theory: If God feels pain, then he puts forth his will to bear and subject that pain; if the pain comes to him from his creature, living in him, will the endurance of God be confined to himself, and not, in its turn, pass beyond the bounds of his individuality, and react upon the sufferer to his sustaining? I do not mean that sustaining which a man feels from knowing his will one with God's and God with him, but such sustaining as those his creatures also may have who do not or cannot know whence the sustaining comes. I believe that the endurance of God goes forth to uphold, that his patience is strength to his creatures, and that, while the whole creation may well groan, its suffering is more bearable therefore than it seems to the repugnance of our regard.'

'That is a dangerous doctrine,' said Clementina.

'Will it then make the cruel man more cruel to be told that God is caring for the tortured creature from the citadel of whose life he would force an answer to save his own from the sphinx that must at last devour him, let him answer ever so wisely? Or will it make the tender less pitiful to be consoled a little in the agony of beholding what they cannot alleviate? Many hearts are from sympathy as sorely in need of comfort as those with whom they suffer. And to such I have one word more – to your heart, my lady, if it will consent to be consoled: The animals, I believe, suffer less than we, because they scarcely think of the past, and not at all of the future – It is the same with children, Mr Graham says; they suffer less than grown people, and for the same reason. To get back something of this privilege of theirs, we have to be obedient and take no thought for the morrow.'[18]

(4) *Our Essential Life: Being the Children of God*

ALIVE, SHARING IN THE SONSHIP OF CHRIST

The life of Jesus is the light of men, revealing to them the Father. But light is not enough; light is for the sake of life. We too must have life in ourselves. We too must, like the Life himself, live. We can live in no way but that in which Jesus lived, in which life was made in him. That way is, to give up our life. This is the one supreme action of life possible to us for the making of life in ourselves. Christ did it of himself, and so became light to us, that we might be able to do it in ourselves, after him, and through his originating act. We must do it ourselves, I say. The help that he has given and gives, the light and the spirit-working of the Lord, the spirit in our hearts, is all in order that we may, as we must, do it ourselves. Till then we are not alive; life is not made in us. The whole strife and labour and agony of the Son with every man, is to get him to die as he died. All preaching that aims not at this, is a building with wood and hay and stubble. If I say not with whole heart, 'My father, do with me as thou wilt, only help me against myself and for thee'; if I cannot say, 'I am thy child, the inheritor of thy spirit, thy being, a part of thyself, glorious in thee, but grown poor in me: let me be thy dog, thy horse, thy anything thou willest; let me be thine in any shape the love that is my Father may please to have me; let me be thine in any way, and my own or another's in no way but thine'; – if we cannot, fully as this, give ourselves to the Father, then we have not yet laid hold upon that for which Christ has laid hold upon us. The faith that a man may, nay, must put in God, reaches above earth and sky, stretches beyond the farthest outlying star of the creatable universe. The question is not at present, however, of removing, mountains, a thing that will one day be simple to us, but of waking and rising from the dead *now*.

When a man truly and perfectly says with Jesus, and as Jesus said it, 'Thy will be done', he closes the everlasting life-circle; the life of the Father and the Son flow through him; he is a part of the divine organism. Then is the prayer of the Lord in him fulfilled: 'I in them and thou in me, that they [may] be made perfect in one.' The Christ in us, is the spirit of the perfect child toward the perfect father. The Christ in us is our own true nature made blossom in us by the Lord, whose life is the light of men that it may become the life of men; for our true nature is childhood to the Father.[19]

BECOMING SONS AND DAUGHTERS
OF OUR HEAVENLY FATHER

Once more I say, the word used by St Paul does not imply that God adopts children that are not his own, but rather that a second time he fathers his own; that a second time they are born – this time from above; that he will make himself tenfold yea, infinitely their father: he will have them back into the very bosom whence they issued, issued that they might learn they could live nowhere else; will have them one with himself. It was for sake of this that, in his Son, he died for them. Let us look at the passage where he reveals use of the word. It is in another of his epistles – that to the Galatians [4:1-7]. 'But I say that so long as the heir is a child differeth nothing from a bondservant, though is lord of all; but is under guardians and stewards until the term appointed of the father. So we also, when we were children, were held in bondage under the rudiments of the world: but when the fulness of time came, God sent forth his Son, born of a woman, born under the law, that he might redeem them which were under the law, that we might receive the adoption of sons. And because ye are sons, God sent forth the Spirit of his into our hearts, crying, Abba, Father. So that Thou art no longer a bond-servant, but a son; and if a son, then an heir through God.'

How could the Revisers choose this last reading, 'an heir through God,' and keep the word adoption? From the passage it is as plain as St Paul could make it, that, by the word translated *adoption,* he means the raising of a father's own child from the condition of tutelage and subjection to others, a state which, he says, is no better than that of a slave, to the position and rights of a son. None but a child could become a son; the idea is – a spiritual coming of age; *only when the child is a man is he really and fully a son.* The thing holds in the earthly relation. How many children of good parents – good children in the main too – never know those parents, never feel towards them as children might, until, grown up, they have left the house – until, perhaps, they are parents themselves, or are parted from them by death! To be a child is not necessarily to be a son or daughter. The childship is the lower condition of the upward process towards the sonship, the soil out of which the true sonship shall grow, the former without which the latter were impossible. God can no more than an earthly parent be content to have only children: he must have sons and daughters – children of his soul, of his spirit, of his love – not merely in the sense that he loves them, or even that they love him, but in the sense that they love like he loves. For this he does not adopt them; he dies to give them himself, thereby to his own to his heart; he gives them a birth from above; they are born again out of himself and into himself – for he is the one and the all. His children are not his real, true sons and daughters until they think like him, feel with him, judge as he judges, are at home with him, and without fear before him because he and they mean the same thing, love same things, seek the same ends. For this we are created; it is the one end of our being, and includes all other ends whatever. It can come only of unbelief and not faith, to make men believe that God has cast them off, repudiated them, said they are not, yea never were, his children – and he all time spending himself to make us the children he designed, foreordained – children who would take him for their Father! He is our father all the time, for he is true; but until we respond with the truth of children, he cannot let all the father out to us; there is no place for the dove of his tenderness to alight. He is our father, but we are not his children. Because we are his children, we must become his sons and daughters. Nothing will satisfy him, or do for us, but that we be one with our father! What else could serve! How else should life ever be a good! Because we are the sons of God, we must become the sons of God.

There may be among my readers – alas for such! to whom the word *Father* brings no cheer, no dawn, in whose heart it rouses no tremble of even a vanished emotion. It is hardly likely to be their fault. For though as children we seldom love up to the mark of reason; though we often offend; and although the conduct of some children is inexplicable to the parent who loves them; yet, if the parent has been but ordinarily kind, even the son who has grown up a worthless man, will now and then feel, in his better moments, some dim reflex of childship, some faintly pleasant, some slightly sorrowful remembrance of the father around whose neck his arms had sometimes clung. In my own childhood and boyhood my father was the refuge from all the ills of life, even sharp pain itself. Therefore I say to son or daughter who has no pleasure in the name *Father*, 'You must interpret the word by all that you have missed in life. Every time a man might have been to you a refuge from the wind, a covert from the tempest, the shadow of a great rock in a weary land, was a time when a father might have been a father indeed. Happy you are yet, if you have found man or woman such a refuge; so far have you known a shadow of the perfect, the only man, the perfect Son of the perfect Father. All that human tenderness can give or desire in the nearness and readiness of love, all and infinitely more must be true of the perfect Father – of the maker of fatherhood, the Father of all the fathers of the earth, specially the Father of those who have specially shown a father-heart.'

This Father would make to himself sons and daughters indeed – that is, such sons and daughters as shall be his sons and daughters not merely by having come from his heart, but by having returned thither – children in virtue of being, such as whence they came, such as choose to be what he is. He will have them share in his being and nature strong wherein he cares for strength; tender and gracious as he is tender and gracious; angry where and as he is angry. Even in the small matter of power, he will have them able to do whatever Son Jesus could on the earth, whose was the life the perfect man, whose works were those of perfect humanity![20]

THE LAST FARTHING

Comment on Jesus' parable: *Verily I say unto thee, thou shalt
by no means come out thence till thou has paid the last farthing*
(Matthew 5: 26).

What special meaning may be read in the different parts of magis-
trate, judge, and officer, beyond the general suggestion, perhaps,
of the tentative approach of the final, I do not know; but I think
I do know what is meant by 'agree on the way', and 'the uttermost
farthing'. The parable is an appeal to the common sense of those
that hear it, in regard to every affair of righteousness. Arrange what
claim lies against you; compulsion waits behind it. Do at once what
you must do one day. As there is no escape from payment, escape at
least the prison that will enforce it. Do not drive justice to extrem-
ities. Duty is imperative; it must be done. It is useless to think to
escape the eternal law of things; yield of yourself, nor compel God
to compel you.

To the honest man, to the man who would fain be honest, the
word is of right gracious import. To the untrue, it is a terrible threat;
to him who is of the truth, it is sweet as most loving promise. He
who is of God's mind in things, rejoices to hear the word of the
changeless Truth; the voice of the Right fills the heavens and the
earth, and makes his soul glad; it is his salvation. If God were not
inexorably just, there would be no stay for the soul of the feeblest
lover of right: 'Thou art true, O Lord: one day I also shall be true!'
'Thou shalt render the right, cost you what it may', is a dread sound
in the ears of those whose life is a falsehood: what but the last farthing
would those who love righteousness more than life pay? It is a joy
profound as peace to know that God is determined upon such payment, is determined to have his children clean, pure as very snow;
is determined that shall they with his help make up for whatever
wrong they have done, but at length be incapable, by eternal choice
of good, under any temptation, of doing the thing that is not divine,
the thing God would not do.

There has been much cherishing of the evil fancy, often without
its taking formal shape, that there is some way of getting out of

the region of strict justice, some mode of managing to escape doing *all* that is required of us; but there is no such escape. A way to avoid any demand of righteousness would be an infinitely worse way than the road to the everlasting fire, for its end would be eternal death. No, there is no escape. There is no heaven with a little of hell in it – no plan to retain this or that of the devil in our hearts or our pockets. Out Satan must go, every hair and feather! Neither shalt thou think to be delivered from the necessity of *being* good by being made good. God is the God of the animals in a far lovelier way, I suspect, than many of us dare to think, but he will not be the God of a man by making a good beast of him. Thou must be good; neither death nor any admittance into good company will make thee good; though, doubtless, if thou be willing and try, these and all other best helps will be given thee. There is no clothing in a robe of imputed righteousness, that poorest of legal cobwebs spun by spiritual spiders. To me it seems like an invention of well-meaning dulness to soothe insanity; and indeed it has proved a door of escape out of worse imaginations. It is apparently an old 'doctrine'; for St John seems to point at it where he says, 'Little children, let no man lead you astray; he that doeth righteousness is righteous even as he is righteous.' Christ is our righteousness, not that we should escape punishment, still less escape being righteous, but as the live potent creator of righteousness in us, so that we, with our wills receiving his spirit, shall like him resist unto blood, striving against sin; shall know in ourselves, as he knows, what a lovely thing is righteousness, what a mean, ugly, unnatural thing is unrighteousness. He *is* our righteousness, and that righteousness is no fiction, no pretence, no imputation.

One thing that tends to keep men from seeing righteousness and unrighteousness as they are, is, that they have been told many things are righteous and unrighteous, which are neither the one nor the other. Righteousness is just fairness – from God to man, from man to God and to man; it is giving every one his due – his large mighty due. He is righteous, and no one else, who does this. And any system which tends to persuade men that there is any salvation but that of becoming righteous even as Jesus is righteous; that a man can be made good, as a good dog is good, without his own willed share in the making; that a man is saved by having his sins hidden under a robe of imputed righteousness – that system, so far as this tendency, is of the devil and not of God. Thank God, not even error shall injure the true of heart; it is not wickedness. They grow in the truth, and as love casts out fear, so truth casts out false-hood. I read then, in this parable, that a man had better make up his mind to be righteous, to be fair, to do what he can to pay what he owes, in any and all the relations of life – all the matters, in a word, wherein one man may demand of another, or complain that he has not received fair play. Arrange your matters with those who have anything against you, while you are yet together and things have not gone too far to be arranged; *you will have to do it,* and that under less easy circumstances than now. Putting off is of no use. You must. The thing has to be done; there are means of compelling you.[21]

WHERE WE GET OUR IDEAS OF GOD

'I have heard Mr Wingfold say,' returned Dorothy, 'that however men may have been driven to form their ideas of God before Christ came, no man can, with thorough honesty, take the name of a Christian, whose ideas of the Father of men are gathered from any other field than the life, thought, words, deeds, of the only Son of that Father. He says it is not from the Bible as a book that we are to draw our ideas of God, but from the living Man into whose presence that book brings us, Who is alive now, and gives His spirit that they who read about Him may understand what kind of being He is, and why He did as He did, and know Him, in some possible measure, as He knows Himself.

'A man may look another in the face for a hundred years and not know him. Men have looked Jesus Christ in the face, and not known either Him or his Father. It was needful that He should appear, to begin the knowing of Him, but speedily was His visible presence taken away, that it might not become, as assuredly it would have become, a veil to hide from men the Father of their spirits.'[22]

Safe with the Father

The narrator and his father, caught in a snowstorm at night.

It got darker and darker, for the clouds went on gathering, and the snow was coming down in huge dull flakes. Faster and thicker they came, until at length we could see nothing of the road before us, and were compelled to leave all to the wisdom of our horses. My father, having great confidence in his own little mare, which had carried him through many a doubtful and difficult place, rode first. I followed close behind. He kept on talking to me very cheerfully – I have thought since – to prevent me from getting frightened. But I had not a thought of fear. To be with my father was to me perfect safety. He was in the act of telling me how, on more occasions than one, Missy had got him through places where the road was impassable, by walking on the tops of the walls, when all at once both our horses plunged into a gulf of snow. The more my mare struggled, the deeper we sank in it. For a moment I thought it was closing over my head.

'Father! Father!' I shouted.

'Don't be frightened, my boy,' cried my father, his voice seeming to come from far away. 'We are in God's hands. I can't help you now, but as soon as Missy has got quieter, I shall come to you' ...

*   *   *

The narrator and his father still out in the snowstorm,
after having built a small cave out of a peat-stack for protection.

Creeping in, we commenced building up the entrance. We had not proceeded far, however, before we found that our cave was too small, and that as we should have to remain in it for hours, we must find it very cramped. Therefore, instead of using any more of the peats already pulled out, we finished building up the wall with others fresh drawn from the inside. When at length we had, to the best of our ability, completed our immuring, we sat down to wait for the morning – my father as calm as if he had been seated in his study-

chair, and I in a state of condensed delight; for was not this a grand
adventure – with my father to share it, and keep it from going too far?
He sat with his back leaning against the side of the hole, and I sat
between his knees, and leaned against him. His arms were folded
round me; and could ever boy be more blessed than I was then?
The sense of outside danger; the knowledge that if the wind rose, we
might be walled up in snow before the morning; the assurance of
present safety and good hope – all made such an impression upon my
mind that ever since when any trouble has threatened me, I have
invariably turned first in thought to the memory of that harbour of
refuge from the storm. There I sat for long hours secure in my
father's arms, and knew that the soundless snow was falling thick
around us, and marked occasionally the threatening wail of the
wind like the cry of a wild beast scenting us from afar ...

*　*　*

Later, the narrator and his father
still in the peat stack during a snowstorm.

'This nest which we have made to shelter us,' he resumed, 'brings to
my mind what the Psalmist says about dwelling in the secret place
of the Most High. Everyone who will, may there, like the swallow,
make himself a nest.'

'This can't be very like that, though, surely, father,' I ventured to
object.

'Why not, my boy?'

'It's not safe enough, for one thing.'

'You are right there. Still it is like. It is our place of refuge.'

'The cold does get through it, father.'

'But it keeps our minds at peace. Even the refuge in God does not
always secure us from external suffering. The heart may be quite
happy and strong when the hands are benumbed with cold. Yes,
the heart even may grow cold with coming death, while the man
himself retreats the farther into the secret place of the Most High,
growing more calm and hopeful as the last cold invades the house of

his body. I believe that all troubles come to drive us into that refuge – that secret place where alone we can be safe.'

I could easily have waked him, but I was not selfish enough for that: I sat still and shivered and felt very dreary. Then the last words of my father began to return upon me, and with a throb or relief, the thought awoke in my mind that although my father was asleep, the great Father of us both, he in whose heart lay that secret place of refuge, neither slumbered nor slept. And now I was able to wait in patience, with an idea, if not a sense of the present care of God, such as I had never had before. When, after some years, my father was taken from us, the thought of this night came again and again, and I would say in my heart: 'My father sleeps that I may know the better that The Father wakes.'[23]

OUR FATHER'S FATHER

One young woman, Margaret, responding to another's inquiry
as to how she had been able to respond without jealousy
over the lost love of a man, especially since she could not confide
about it to her own father who had died.

' … But you must have loved him dreadfully.'

'Perhaps I did. But I had no anxiety about it.'

'But that you could not leave to a father such as yours even to settle.'

'No. But I could to God. I could trust God with what I could not speak to my father about. He is my father's father, you know; and so, more to him and me than we could be to each other. The more we love God, the more we love each other; for we find he makes the very love which sometimes we foolishly fear to do injustice to, by loving him most. I love my father ten times more because he loves God, and because God has secrets with him.'

'I wish God were a father to me as he is to you Margaret.'

'But he is your father, whether you wish it or not. He cannot be more your father than he is. You may be more his child than you are, but not more than he meant you to be, nor more than he made you for. You are infinitely more his child than you have grown to yet. He made you altogether his child, but you have not given in to it yet.'

'Oh! yes; I know what you mean. I feel it is true.'

'The Prodigal Son was his father's child. He knew it, and gave in to it. He did not say: "I wish my father loved me enough to treat me like a child again." He did not say that, but – I will arise and go to my father.'

Euphra made no answer but wept. Margaret said no more.[24]

(5) *The Truth in Christ*

TRUE FAITH: KNOWING HIM
BY OBEYING HIM

What I insist upon is, that a man's faith shall be in the living, loving, ruling, helping Christ, devoted to us as much as ever he was, and with all the powers of the Godhead for the salvation of his brethren. It is not faith that he did this, that his work wrought that – it is faith in the man who did and is doing everything for us that will save him. Without this he cannot work to heal spiritually, any more than he would heal physically, when he was present to the eyes of men. Do you ask, 'What is faith in him?' I answer, The leaving of your way, your objects, your self, and the taking of his and him; the leaving of your trust in men, in money, in opinion, in character, in atonement itself, and *doing as he tells you.* I can find no words strong enough to serve for the weight of this necessity – this obedience. It is the one terrible heresy of the church, that it has always been presenting something else than obedience as faith in Christ. The work of Christ is not the Working Christ, any more than the clothing of Christ is the Body of Christ. If the woman who touched the hem of his garment had trusted in the garment and not in him who wore it, would she have been healed? And the reason that so many who believe *about* Christ rather than in him, get the comfort they do, is that, touching thus the mere hem of his garment, they cannot help believing a little in the live man inside the garment. It is not wonderful that such believers should so often be miserable; they lay themselves down to sleep with nothing but the skirt of his robe in their hand – a robe too, I say, that never was his, only by them is supposed his – when they might sleep in peace with the living Lord in their hearts. Instead of so knowing Christ that they have him in them saving them, they lie wasting themselves in soul-sickening self-examination as to whether they are believers, whether they are really trusting in the atonement, whether they are truly sorry for their sins – the way to madness of the brain, and despair of the heart. Some even ponder the imponderable – whether they are of the elect, whether they have an interest in the blood shed for sin, whether theirs is a saving faith – when all the time the man who died for them is waiting to begin to save them from every evil – and first from this self which is consuming them with trouble about its salvation; he will set them free, and take them home to the bosom of the Father – if only they will mind what he says to them – which is the beginning, middle, and end of faith. If, instead of searching into the mysteries of corruption in their own charnel-houses, they would but awake and arise from the dead, and come out into the light which Christ is waiting to give them, he would begin at once to fill them with the fulness of God.

'But I do not know how to awake and arise!' I will tell you: – Get up, and do something the master tells you; so make yourself his disciple at once. Instead of asking yourself whether you believe or not, ask yourself whether you have this day done one thing because he said, Do it, or once abstained because he said, Do not do it. It is simply absurd to say you believe or even want to believe in him, if you do not anything he tells you. If you can think of nothing he ever said as having had an atom of influence on your doing or not doing, you have too good ground to consider yourself no disciple of his. Do not, I pray you, worse than waste your time in trying to convince yourself that you are his disciple notwithstanding – that for this reason or that you still have cause to think you believe in him. What, though you should succeed in persuading yourself to absolute certainty that you are his disciple, if, after all, he say to you, 'Why did you not do the things I told you? Depart from me; I do not know you!' Instead of trying to persuade yourself, if the thing be true you can make it truer; if it be not true, you can begin at once to make it true, to be a disciple of the Living One – by obeying him in the first thing you can think of in which you are not obeying him. We must learn to obey him in everything, and so must begin somewhere: let it be at once, and in the very next thing that lies at the door of our conscience! Oh, fools and slow of heart, if you think of nothing but Christ, and do not set yourselves to do his words! you but build your houses on the sand. What have such teachers not to answer for who have turned your regard away from the direct words of the Lord himself, which are spirit and life, to contemplate plans of salvation tortured out of the words of his apostles, even were those plans as true as they are false! There is but one plan of salvation, and that is to believe in the Lord Jesus Christ; that is, to take him for what he is – our master, and his words as if he meant them, which assuredly he did. To do his words is to enter into vital relation with him, obey him is the only way to be one with him. The relation between him and us is an absolute one; it can nohow begin to *live* but in obedience, it *is* obedience.[25]

THE BIBLE
LEADS US TO JESUS CHRIST

But to the man who would live throughout the whole divine form of his being, not confining himself to one broken corner of his kingdom, and leaving the rest to the demons that haunt such deserts, a thousand questions will arise to which the Bible does not even allude. Has he indeed nothing to do with such? Do they lie beyond the sphere of his responsibility? 'Leave them,' says the dull disciple. 'I cannot,' returns the man. 'Not only does that degree of peace of mind without which action is impossible, depend upon the answers to these questions, but my conduct itself must correspond to these answers.' 'Leave them at least till God chooses to explain, if he ever will.' 'No. Questions imply answers. He has put the questions in my heart; he holds the answers in his. I will seek them from him. I will wait, but not till I have knocked. I will be patient, but not till I have asked. I will seek until I find. He has something for me. My prayer shall go up unto the God of my life.'

Sad, indeed, would the whole matter be, if the Bible had told us *everything* God meant us to believe. But herein is the Bible itself greatly wronged. It nowhere lays claim to be regarded as *the* Word, *the* Way, *the* Truth. The Bible leads us to Jesus, the inexhaustible, the ever unfolding *Revelation* of God. It is Christ 'in whom are *hid* all the treasures of wisdom and knowledge,' not the Bible, save as leading to him. And why are we told that these treasures are hid in him who is the Revelation of God? Is it that we should despair of finding them and cease to seek them? Are they not hid in him that they may be revealed to us in due time – that is, when we are in need of them? Is not their hiding in him the mediatorial step towards their unfolding in us? Is he not the Truth? the Truth to men? Is he not the High Priest of his brethren, to answer all the troubled questionings that arise in their dim humanity? For it is his heart which 'contains of good, wise, just, the perfect shape'.

Didymus answers, 'No doubt; what we know not now, we shall know hereafter.' Certainly there may be things which the mere passing into another stage of existence will illuminate; but the questions that come here, must be inquired into here, and if not answered here, then there too until they be answered. There is more hid in Christ than we shall ever learn, here or there either; but they that begin first to inquire will soonest be gladdened with revelation; and with them he will be best pleased, for the slowness of his disciples troubled him of old. To say that we must wait for the other world, to know the mind of him who came to this world to give himself to us, seems to me the foolishness of a worldly and lazy spirit. The Son of God *is* the Teacher of men, giving to them of his Spirit – that Spirit which manifests the deep things of God, being to a man the mind of Christ. The great heresy of the Church of the present day is unbelief in this Spirit.[26]

ASKING, TRUSTING, BELIEVING
IN JESUS

What should I think of my child, if I found that he limited his faith in me and hope from me to the few promises he had heard me utter! The faith that limits itself to the promises of God, seems to me to partake of the paltry character of such a faith in my child – good enough for a Pagan, but for a Christian a miserable and wretched faith. Those who rest in such a faith would feel yet more comfortable if they had God's bond instead of his word, which they regard not as the outcome of his character, but as a pledge of his honour. They try to believe in the truth of his word, but the truth of his Being, they understand not. In his oath they persuade themselves that they put confidence: in *himself* they do not believe, for they know him not. Therefore it is little wonder that they distrust those swellings of the heart which are his drawings of the man towards him, as sun and moon heave the ocean mass heavenward. Brother, sister, if such is your faith, you will not, must not stop there. You must come out of this bondage of the law to which you give the name of grace, for there is little that is gracious in it. You will yet know the dignity of your high calling, and the love of God that passeth knowledge. He is not afraid of your presumptuous approach to him. It is you who are afraid to come near him. He is not watching over his dignity. It is you who fear to be sent away as the disciples would have sent away the little children. It is you who think so much about your souls and are so afraid of losing your life, that you dare not draw near to the Life of life, lest it should consume you.

Our God, we will trust thee. Shall we not find thee equal to our faith? One day, we shall laugh ourselves to scorn that we looked for so little from thee; for thy giving will not be limited by our hoping.

O thou of little faith! 'in everything', – I am quoting our own Bible; nay, more, I am quoting a divine soul that knew his master Christ, and in his strength opposed apostles, not to say Christians, to their faces, because they could not believe more than a little in God; could believe only for themselves and not for their fellows; could believe for the few of the chosen nation for whom they had

God's ancient word, but could not believe for the multitude of the nations, for the millions of hearts that God had made to search after him and find him, – 'In everything,' says St Paul, 'in everything, by prayer and supplication, with thanksgiving, let your requests be made known unto God.' For this *everything,* nothing is too small. That it should trouble us is enough – There is some principle involved in it worth the notice even of God himself, for did he not make us so that the thing does trouble us? And surely for this *everything,* nothing can be too great. When the Son of man cometh and findeth too much faith on the earth – may God in his mercy slay us. Meantime, we will hope and trust.[27]

WHAT IS A CHRISTIAN?

What is Christianity? I know but one definition, the analysis of which, if the thing in question be a truth, must be the joyous labour of every devout heart to all eternity. For Christianity does not mean what you think or what I think concerning Christ, but what is *of* Christ. My Christianity, if ever I come to have any, will be what of Christ is in me; your Christianity now is what of Christ is in you. Last Sunday I showed you our Lord's very words – that he, and no other, was his disciple who did what he told him – and said, therefore, that I dared not call myself a disciple. I say the same thing in saying now that I dare not call myself a Christian, lest I should offend him with my 'Lord, Lord!' Still it is, and I cannot now help it, in the name of Christianity that I here stand. I have – alas! with blameful and appalling thoughtlessness! – subscribed my name, as a believer, to the articles of the Church of England, with no better reason than that I was unaware of any dissent therefrom, and have been ordained one of her ministers. The relations into which this has brought me I do not feel justified in severing at once, lest I should therein seem to deny that which its own illumination may yet show me to be true, and I desire therefore a little respite and room for thought and resolve. But meantime it remains my business, as an honest man in the employment of the church, to do my best towards the setting forth of the claims of him upon whom that church is founded, and in whose name she exists. As one standing on the outskirts of a listening Galilean crowd, a word comes now and then to my hungry ears and hungrier heart: I turn and tell it again to you – not that ye have not heard it also, but that I may stir you up to ask yourselves: 'Do I then obey this word? Have I ever, have I once, sought to obey it? Am I a pupil of Jesus? Am I a Christian?' Hear then of his words. For me, they fill my heart with doubt and dismay!

The Lord says, *Love your enemies.* Sayest thou, *It is impossible?* Then dost thou mock the word of him who said, *I am the Truth,* and hast no part in him. Sayest thou, *Alas! I cannot?* Thou sayest true, I doubt not. But hast thou tried whether he who made will not increase the strength put forth to obey him?

The Lord says, *Be ye perfect.* Dost thou then aim after perfection, or dost thou excuse thy wilful shortcomings, and say *To err is human* – nor hopest that it may also be found human to grow divine? Then ask thyself, for thou hast good cause, whether thou hast any part in him.

The Lord said, *Lay not up for yourselves treasures on earth.* My part is not now to preach against the love of money, but to ask you, *Are you laying up for yourselves treasures on earth?* As to what the command means, the honest heart and the dishonest must each settle it in his own way; but if your heart condemn you, what I have to say is, Call not yourselves Christians, but consider whether you ought not to become disciples indeed. No doubt you can instance this, that, and the other man who does as you do, and of whom yet no man dreams of questioning the Christianity: it matters not a hair; all that goes but to say that you are pagans together. Do not mistake me: I judge you not. But I ask you, as mouth-piece most unworthy of that Christianity in the name of which this building stands and we are met therein, to judge your own selves by the words of its founder.

The Lord said, *Take no thought for your life. Take no thought for the morrow.* Explain it as you may or can; but ask yourselves, Do I take no thought for my life? Do I take no thought for the morrow? and answer to yourselves whether or no ye are Christians.

The Lord says, *Judge not.* Didst thou judge thy neighbour yesterday? Wilt thou judge him again to-morrow? Art thou judging him now in the very heart that within thy bosom sits hearing the words

Judge not? Or wilt thou ask yet again, Who is my neighbour? How then canst thou look to be of those that shall enter through the gates into the city? I tell thee not, for I profess not yet to know anything, but doth not thine own profession of Christianity counsel thee to fall upon thy face, and cry to him whom thou mockest, 'I am a sinful man, O Lord'?

The Lord said, *All things whatsoever ye would that men should do to you, do ye even so to them.* Ye that buy and sell, do you obey this law? Examine yourselves and see. Ye would that men should deal fairly by you: do you deal fairly by them as ye would count fairness in them to you? If conscience makes you hang the head inwardly, however you sit with it erect in the pew, dare you add to your crime against the law and the prophets the insult to Christ of calling yourselves his disciples?

Not every one that saith unto me, Lord, Lord, shall enter into the kingdom of heaven, but he that doeth the will of my Father which is in heaven. He will none but those who with him do the will of the Father.'[28]

BOUND TO OBEY THE TRUTH

As much as ever he believed Dorothy mistaken, and yet could have kneeled in reverence before her. He had himself tried to do the truth, and no one but he who tries to do the truth can perceive the grandeur of another who does the same. Alive to his own shortcomings, such a one the better understands the success of his brother or sister: there the truth takes to him shape, and he worships at her shrine. He saw more clearly than before what he had been learning ever since she had renounced him, that it is not correctness of opinion – could he be sure that his own opinions were correct? – that constitutes rightness, but that condition of soul which, as a matter of course, causes it to move along the lines of truth and duty – the life going forth in motion according to the law of light: this alone places a nature in harmony with the eternal Truth. It was in the doing of the will of His Father that Jesus was the Son of God – yea, the eternal Son of the eternal Father. Nor was this to make little of the truth intellectually considered – of the fact of things. The greatest fact of all is that we are bound to obey the truth, and that to the full extent of our knowledge thereof, however little that may be. This obligation acknowledged and obeyed, the road is open to all truth – and the only road. The way to know is to do the known. Then why, thought Richard with himself, should he and Dorothy be parted? Why should Dorothy imagine they should? All depended on their common magnanimity, not the magnanimity that pardons faults, but the magnanimity that recognises virtues. He who gladly kneels with one who thinks largely wide from himself, in so doing draws nearer to the Father of both than he who pours forth his soul in sympathetic torrent only in the company of those who think like himself. If a man be of the truth, then and only then is he of those who gather with the Lord.[29]

A Spiritual Journey

The dwarf, Polwarth, recounting for Curate Thomas Wingfold
his own spiritual story.

' ... but the next thought of which I was aware was, What if I misunderstood God the same way the boy had misunderstood me! and the next thing was to take my New Testament from the shelf on which I had laid it aside.

'Another evening of that same summer, I said to myself that I would begin at the beginning and read it through. I had no definite idea in the resolve; it seemed a good thing to do, and I would do it. It would serve towards keeping up my connection in a way with things above. I began, but did not that night get through the first chapter of St Matthew. Conscientiously I read every word of the genealogy, but when I came to the twenty-third verse and read, "Thou shalt call his name JESUS; for he shall save his people from their sins," I fell on my knees. No system of theology had come between me and a common sense reading of the book. I did not for a moment imagine that to be saved from my sins meant to be saved from the punishment of them. That would have been no glad tidings to me. My sinfulness was ever before me, and often my sins too, and loved them not, yet could not free myself of them. They were

in me and of me, and how was I to part myself from that which
came to me with my consciousness, which asserted itself in me as
one with my consciousness? I could not get behind myself so as to
reach its root. But here was news of one who came from behind
that root itself to deliver me from that in me which made being a
bad thing! ...

'To tell you all that followed, if I could recall and narrate it in
order, would take hours. Suffice it that from that moment I was a
student, a disciple. Soon to me also came then the two questions: *How
do I know that there is a God at all?* and *How am I to know that such a
man as Jesus ever lived?* I could answer neither. But in the meantime
I was reading the story – was drawn to the Man there presented, and
was trying to understand his being, and character, and principles of
life and action. And to sum all in a word, many months had not
passed ere I had forgotten to seek an answer to either question: they
were in fact questions no longer: I had seen the man Jesus Christ, and
in him had known the Father of him and of me. My dear sir, no
conviction can be got, or if it could be got, would be of any sufficing
value, through that dealer in second-hand goods, the intellect. If
by it we could prove there is a God, it would be of small avail
indeed: we must see him and know him, to know that he was not a
demon. But I know no other way of knowing that there is a God but
that which reveals what he is – the only idea that could be God –
shows him in his own self-proving existence – and that way is Jesus
Christ as he revealed himself on earth, and as he is revealed afresh to
every heart that seeks to know the truth concerning him.'

A pause followed – a solemn one – and then again Polwarth spoke.

'Either the whole frame of existence,' he said, 'is a wretched, miserable unfitness, a chaos with dreams of a world, a chaos in which the
higher is for ever subject to the lower, or it is an embodied idea
growing towards perfection in him who is the one perfect creative
Idea, the Father of lights who suffers himself that he may bring his
many sons into the glory which is his own glory.'[30]

(6) *God's Good Purposes for Our Lives*

TO BEHOLD THE FACE OF THE CREATOR

Reflections on Matthew 5: 8 –
Blessed are the pure in heart for they shall see God.

The cry of the deepest in man has always been, to see God. It was the cry of Moses and the cry of Job, the cry of psalmist and of prophet; and to the cry, there has ever been faintly heard a far approach of coming answer. In the fullness of time the Son appears with the proclamation that a certain class of men shall behold the Father: 'Blessed are the pure in heart,' he cries, 'for they shall see God.' He who saw God, who sees him now, who always did and always will see him, says, 'Be pure, and you also shall see him'. To see God was the Lord's own, eternal, one happiness; therefore he knew that the essential bliss of the creature is to behold the face of the creator. In that face lies the mystery of a man's own nature, the history of a man's own being. He who can read no line of it, can know neither himself nor his fellow; he only who knows God a little, can at all understand man. The blessed in Dante's Paradise ever and always read each other's thoughts in God. Looking to him, they find their neighbour. All that the creature needs to see or know, all that the creature can see or know, is the face of him from whom he came. Not seeing and knowing it, he will never be at rest; seeing and knowing it, his existence will yet indeed be a mystery to him and an awe, but no more a dismay. To know that it is, and that it has power neither to continue nor to cease, must to any soul alive enough to appreciate the fact, be merest terror, save also it knows one with it the Power by which it exists. From the man who comes to know and feel that Power in him and one with him, loneliness, anxiety, and fear vanish; he is no more an orphan without a home, a little one astray on the cold waste of a helpless consciousness ...

None but the pure in heart see God; only the growing pure hope to see him. Even those who saw the Lord, the express image of his person, did not see God. They only saw Jesus – and then but the outside Jesus, or a little more. They were not pure in heart; they saw him and did not see him. They saw him with their eyes, but not with those eyes which alone can see God. Those were not born in them yet. Neither the eyes of the resurrection-body, nor the eyes of unembodied spirits can see God; only the eyes of that eternal something that is of the very essence of God, the thought-eyes, the truth-eyes, the love-eyes, can see him. It is not because we are created and he uncreated, it is not because of any difference involved in that difference of all differences that we cannot see him. If he pleased to take a shape, and that shape were presented to us, and we saw that shape, we should not therefore be seeing God. Even if we knew it was a shape of God – call it even God himself our eyes rested upon; if we had been told the fact and believed the report; yet, if we did not see the *Godness,* were not capable of recognizing him, so as without the report to know the vision [of] him, we should not be seeing God, we should only be seeing the tabernacle in which for the moment he dwelt. In other words, not seeing what in the form made it a form fit for him to take, we should not be seeing a presence which could only be God.

To see God is to stand on the highest point of created being. Not until we see God – no partial and passing embodiment of him, but the abiding presence – do we stand upon our own mountain-top, the height of the existence God has given us, and up to which he is leading us. That there we should stand, is the end of our creation. This truth is at the heart of everything, means all kinds of completions, may be uttered in many ways; but language will never compass it, for form will never contain it.

Nor shall we ever see, that is know God perfectly. We shall indeed never absolutely know man or woman or child; but we may know God as we never can know human being – as never can know ourselves. We not only may, but we must so know him, and it can never be until we are pure in heart. Then shall we know him with the infinitude of an ever-growing knowledge.[31]

Affirming Our Share
in the Divine Sonship of Jesus

Because we are come out of the divine nature, which chooses to be divine, we must choose to be divine, to be of God, to be one with God, loving and living as he loves and lives, and so be partakers of the divine nature, or we perish. Man cannot originate this life; it must be shown him, and he must choose it. God is the father of Jesus and of us – of every possibility of our being; but while God is the father of his children, Jesus is the father of their sonship; for in him is made the life which is sonship to the Father – the recognition, namely, in fact and life, that the Father has his claim upon his sons and daughters. We are not and cannot become true sons without our will willing his will, our doing following his making. It is the will of Jesus to be the thing God willed and meant him, that made him the true son of God. He was not the son of God because he could not help it, but because he willed to be in himself the son that he was in the divine idea. So with us: we must *be* the sons we are. We are not made to be what we cannot help being; sons and daughters are not after such fashion! We are sons and daughters in God's claim; we must be sons and daughters in our will. And we can be sons and daughters, saved into the original necessity and eternal bliss of our being, only by choosing God for the father he is, and doing his will – yielding ourselves true sons to the absolute Father. Therein lies human bliss – only and essential. The working out of this our salvation must be pain, and the handing of it down to them that are below must ever be in pain; but the eternal form of the will of God in and for us, is intensity of bliss.

'And the life was the light of men.'

The life of which I have now spoken became light to men in the appearing of him in whom it came into being. The life became light that men might see it, and themselves live by choosing that life also, by choosing so to live, such to be.

There is always something deeper than anything said – a something of which all human, all divine words, figures, pictures, motion-forms, are but the outer laminar spheres through which the central reality shines more or less plainly. Light itself is but the poor outside form of a deeper, better thing, namely life. The life is Christ. The light too is Christ, but only the body of Christ. The life is Christ himself. The light is what we *see* and shall see in him; the life is what we may *be* in him. The life 'is a light by abundant clarity invisible'; it is the unspeakable unknown; it must become light such as men can see before men can know it. Therefore the obedient human God appeared as the obedient divine man, doing the works of his father – the things, that is, which his father did – doing them humbly before unfriendly brethren. The Son of the Father must take his own form in the substance of flesh, that he may be seen of men, and so become the light of men – not that men may have light, but that men may have life; – that, seeing what they could not originate, they may, through the life that is in them, begin to hunger after the life of which they are capable, and which is essential to their being; – that the life in them may long for him who is their life and thirst for its own perfection, even as root and stem may thirst for the flower for whose sake, and through whose presence in them, they exist. That the child of God may become the son of God by beholding *the* Son, the life revealed in light; that the radiant heart of the Son of God may be the sunlight to his fellows; that the idea may be drawn out by the presence and drawing of the Ideal, the perfect Son of the Father, was sent to his brethren.[32]

LIFE IN TOGETHERNESS WITH GOD

The soul compact of harmonies has more life, a larger being, than the soul consumed of cares; the sage is a larger life than the clown; the poet is more alive than the man whose life flows out that money may come in; the man who loves his fellow is infinitely more alive than he whose endeavour is to exalt himself above him; the man who strives to be better, than he who longs for the praise of the many; but the man to whom God is all in all, who feels his life-roots, hid with Christ in God, who knows himself the inheritor of all wealth and worlds and ages, yea, of power essential and in itself, that man has begun to be alive indeed.

Let us in all the troubles of life remember – that our one lack is life – that what we need is more life – more of the life-making presence in us making us more, and more largely, alive. When most oppressed, when most weary of life, as our unbelief would phrase it, let us bethink ourselves that it is in truth the inroad and presence of death we are weary of. When most inclined to sleep let us rouse ourselves to live. Of all things let us avoid the false refuge of a weary collapse, a hopeless yielding to things as they are. It is the life in us that is discontented; we need more of what is discontented, not more of the cause of its discontent. Discontent, I repeat, is the life in us that has not enough of itself, is not enough to itself, so calls for more. He has the victory who, in the midst of pain and weakness, cries out, not for death, not for the repose of forgetfulness, but for strength to fight; for more power, more consciousness of being, more God in him ...

To believe in God our strength in the face of all seeming denial, to believe in him out of the heart of weakness and unbelief, in spite of numbness and weariness and lethargy; to believe in the wide-awake real, through all the stupefying, enervating, distorting dream; to will to wake, when the very being seems athirst for a godless repose; – these are the broken steps up to the high fields where repose is but a form of strength, strength but a form of joy, joy but a form of love. 'I am weak,' says the true soul, 'but not so weak that I would not be strong; not so sleepy that I would not see the sun rise; not so lame but that I would walk! Thanks be to him who perfects strength in weakness, and gives to his beloved while they sleep!'

If we will but let our God and Father work his will with us, there can be no limit to his enlargement of our existence, to the flood of life with which he will overflow our consciousness. We have no conception of what life might be, of how vast the consciousness of which we could be made capable. Many can recall some moment in which life seemed richer and fuller than ever before; to some, such moments arrive mostly in dreams: shall soul, awake or asleep, infold a bliss greater than its Life, the living God, can seal, perpetuate, enlarge? Can the human twilight of a dream be capable of generating or holding a fuller life than the morning of divine activity? Surely God could at any moment give to a soul, by a word to that soul, by breathing afresh into the secret caves of its being, a sense of life before which the most exultant ecstasy of earthly triumph would pale to ashes! If ever sunlit, sail-crowded sea, under blue heaven flecked with wind-chased white, filled your soul as with a new gift of life, think what sense of existence must be yours, if he whose thought has but fringed its garment with the outburst of such a show, take his abode with you, and while thinking the gladness of a God inside your being, let you know and feel that he is carrying you as a father in his bosom![33]

Made for What We Must Become

'Mary,' he said again, taking her little hand in his two long, bony ones, 'I love you, my child, to that degree I can not say; and I want you, I do want you, to be a Christian.'

'So do I, father dear,' answered Mary simply, the tears rushing into her eyes at the thought that perhaps she was not one; 'I want me to be a Christian.'

'Yes, my love,' he went on; 'but it is not that I do not think you a Christian; it is that I want you to be a downright real Christian, not one that is but trying to feel as a Christian ought to feel. I have lost so much precious time in that way!'

'Tell me – tell me,' cried Mary, clasping her other hand over his. 'What would you have me do?'

'I will tell you. I am just trying now,' he responded. 'A Christian is just one that does what the Lord Jesus tells him. Neither more nor less than that makes a Christian. It is not even understanding the Lord Jesus that makes one a Christian. That makes one dear to the Father; but it is being a Christian, that is, doing what he tells us, that makes us understand him. Peter says the Holy Spirit is given to them that obey him: what else is that but just actually, really, doing what he says – just as if I was to tell you to go and fetch my Bible, and you would get up and go? Did you ever do anything, my child, just because Jesus told you to do it?'

Mary did not answer immediately. She thought awhile. Then she spoke. 'Yes, father,' she said, 'I think so. Two nights ago, George was very rude to me – I don't mean anything bad, but you know he is very rough.'

'I know it, my child. And you must not think I don't care because I think it better not to interfere. I am with you all the time.'

'Thank you, father; I know it. Well, when I was going to bed, I was angry with him still so it was no wonder I found I could not say my prayers. Then I remembered how Jesus said we must forgive or we should not be forgiven. So I forgave him with all my heart, and kindly, too, and then I found I could pray.'

The father stretched out his arm and drew her to his bosom, murmuring, 'My child! my Christ's child!' After a little he began to talk again.

'It is a miserable thing to hear those who desire to believe themselves Christians, talking and talking about this question and that, the discussion of which is all for strife and nowise for unity – not a thought among them of the one command of Christ, to love one another. I fear some are hardly content with not hating those who differ from them.'

'I am sure, father, I try – and I think I do love everybody that loves him,' said Mary.

'Well, that is much – not enough though, my child. We must be like Jesus, and you know that it was while we were yet sinners that Christ died for us; therefore we must love all men, whether they are Christians or not.'

'Tell me, then, what you want me to do, father dear. I will do whatever you tell me.'

'I want you to be just like that to the Lord Christ, Mary. I want you to look out for his will, and find it, and do it. I want you not only to do it, though that is the main thing, when you think of it, but to look for it, that you may do it. I need not say to you that this is not a thing to be talked about much, for you don't do that. You may think me very silent, my love; but I do not talk always when I am inclined, for the fear I might let my feeling out that way, instead of doing something he wants of me with it. And how repulsive and full of offense those generally are who talk most! Our strength ought to go into conduct, not into talk – least of all, into talk about what they call the doctrines of the gospel. The man who does what God tells him, sits at his Father's feet, and looks up in his Father's face; and men had better leave him alone, for he can not greatly mistake his Father, and certainly will not displease him. Look for the lovely will, my child, that you may be its servant, its priest, its sister, its queen, its slave – as Paul calls himself. How that man did glory in his Master !'

'I will try, father,' returned Mary, with a burst of tears. 'I do want to be good. I do want to be one of his slaves, if I may.'

'*May!* my child? You are bound to be. You have no choice but choose it. It is what we are made for – freedom, the divine nature, God's life, a grand, pure, open-eyed existence! It is what Christ died for. You must not talk about may; it is all must.'[34]

BEYOND WHAT KINDNESS CAN DO

There are tender-hearted people who virtually object to the whole scheme of creation; they would neither have force used nor pain suffered; they talk as if kindness could do everything, even where it is not felt. Millions of human beings but for suffering would never develop an atom of affection. The man who would spare *due* suffering is not wise. It is folly to conclude a thing ought not to be done because it hurts. There are powers to be born, creations to be perfected, sinners to be redeemed, through the ministry of pain, that could be born, perfected, redeemed in no other way.[35]

PEACE IN CHRIST

Wingfold's sermon
on behalf of one of his suffering parishioners
about Jesus' own words.

And of all words that ever were spoken, were ever words gentler, tenderer, humbler, lovelier – if true, or more arrogant, man-degrading, God-defying – if false, than these concerning which, as his, I now desire to speak to you: '*Come unto me, all ye that labour and are heavy-laden, and I will give you rest. Take my yoke upon you and learn of me; for*

I am meek and lowly in heart and ye shall find rest unto your souls. For my yoke is easy, and my burden is light.'

Surely these words, could they but be heartily believed, are such as every human heart might gladly hear! What man is there who has not had, has not now, or will not have to class himself amongst the weary and heavy-laden? Ye – who call yourselves Christians profess to believe such rest is to be had, yet how many of you go bowed to the very earth and take no single step towards him who says *'Come,* lift not an eye to see whether a face of mercy may not be looking down upon you!' Is it that, after all, you do not believe there ever was such a man as they call Jesus? That can hardly be. There are few so ignorant or so wilfully illogical as to be able to disbelieve in the existence of the man, or that he spoke words to this effect. Is it then that you are doubtful concerning the whole import of his appearance? In that case, were it but as a doubtful medicine, would it not be well to make some trial of the offer made? If the man said the words, he must have at least believed that he could fulfil them. Who that knows anything of him at all can for a moment hold that this man spoke what he did not believe? The best of the Jews, who yet do not believe in him, say of him that he was a good though mistaken man. Will a man lie for the privilege of being despised and rejected of men, a man of sorrows and acquainted with grief? What but the confidence of truth could have sustained him when he knew that even those who loved him would have left him had they believed what he told them of his coming fate? But then: believing what he said, might he not have been mistaken? A man can hardly be mistaken as to whether he is at peace or not – whether he has rest in his soul or not. Neither, I think, can a man well be mistaken as to whence comes the peace he possesses – as to the well whence he draws his comfort The miser knows his comfort is his gold. Was Jesus likely to be mistaken when he supposed himself to know that his comfort came from his God? Anyhow he believed that his peace came from his obedience – from his oneness with the will of his Father – Friends, if I had such peace as was plainly his, should I not know well whence it came? But I think I hear some one say, 'Doubtless the good man derived comfort from the thought of his Father, but might he not be mistaken in supposing there was any

Father?' Hear me, my friends: I dare not say I know there is a Father. I dare not even say I think; I can only say with my whole heart I hope we have indeed a Father in heaven; but this man says *he knows.* Am I to say he does not know? Can I, who know so much I would gladly have otherwise in myself, imagine him less honest than I am? If he tells me he knows, I am dumb and listen. One I know: *there is,* outweighs a whole creation of voices crying each *I know not, therefore there is not.* And observe it is his own, his own best he wants to give them; no bribe to obedience to his will, but the assurance of bliss if they will do as he does. He wants them to have peace – his peace – peace from the same source whence he has it. For what does he mean by *Take my yoke upon you and learn of me?* He does not mean, *Wear the yoke I lay upon you, and obey my words.* I do not say he might not have said so, or that he does not say what comes to the same thing at other times, but that is not what he says here – that is not the truth he would convey in these words. He means, *Take upon you the yoke I wear; learn to do as I do, who submit everything and refer everything to the will of my Father, yea, have my will only in the carrying out of his: be meek and lowly in heart, and ye shall find rest unto your souls.* With all the grief of humanity in his heart, in the face of the death that awaited him, he yet says, For my yoke, the yoke I wear, is easy, the burden I bear is light. What made that yoke easy – that burden light? That it was the will of the Father. If a man answer, 'Any good man who believed in a God might say as much, and I do not see how it can help me,' my reply is, that this man says *Come unto me, and I will give you rest* – asserting the power to give perfect help to him that comes. Does all this look far away, my friends, and very unlike the things about us? The things about you do not give you peace; from something different you may hope to gain it. And do not our souls themselves fall out with their surroundings, and cry for a nobler, better, more beautiful life?

But someone will perhaps say, 'It is well; but were I meek and lowly in heart as he of whom you speak, it could not touch my trouble: that springs not from myself, but from one whom I love.' I answer, if the peace be the peace of the Son of Man, it must reach to every cause of unrest and if thou hadst it, would it not then be next door to thy friend? How shall he whom thou lovest receive it the most readily but through thee who lovest him? What if thy faith should be the next step to his? Anyhow, if this peace be not an all-reaching as well as heart-filling peace; if it be not a righteous and a lovely peace, and that in despite of all surrounding and opposing troubles, then it is not the peace of God, for that passeth all under-standing: so at least say they who profess to know, and I desire to take them at their word. If thy trouble be a trouble thy God cannot set right, then either thy God is not the true God or there is no true God, and the man who professed to reveal him led the one perfect life in virtue of his faith in a falsehood. Alas! for poor men and women and their aching hearts! – If it offend any of you that I speak of Jesus as the man who professed to reveal God, I answer that the man I see, and he draws me as with the strength of the adorable Truth; but if in him I should certainly find the God for the lack of whose peace I and my brethren and sisters pine, then were heaven itself too narrow to hold my exultation, for in God himself alone could my joy find room.

Come, then, sore heart, and see whether his heart cannot heal thine. He knows what sighs and tears are, and if he knew no sin in himself, the more pitiful must it have been to him to behold the sighs and tears that guilt wrung from the tortured hearts of his brethren and sisters. Brothers, Sisters, we must get rid of this misery of ours. It is slaying us – It is turning the fair earth into a hell, and our hearts into its fuel. There stands the man who says he knows: take him at his word. Go to him who says in the might of his eternal tenderness and his human pity, *Come unto me, all ye that labour and are heavy-laden, and I will give you rest. Take my yoke upon you, and learn of me; for I am meek and lowly in heart: and ye shall find rest unto your souls. For my yoke is easy, and my burden is light.*[36]

(7) *Loving Others as Christ Loved Us*

Love alone fulfills the Law

I am certain that it is impossible to keep the law towards one's neighbour except one loves him. The law itself is infinite, reaching to such delicacies of action, that the man who tries most will be the man most aware of defeat. We are not made for law but for love. Love is law, because it is infinitely more than law. It is of an altogether higher region than law – is, in fact, the creator of law. Had it not been for love, not one of the *shalt-nots* of the law would have been uttered. True, once uttered, they shew themselves in the form of justice, yea, even in the inferior and worldly forms of prudence and self-preservation; but it was love that spoke them first. Were there no love in us, what sense of justice could we have? Would not each be filled with the sense of his own wants, and be for ever tearing to himself? I do not say it is *conscious* love that breeds justice, but I do say that without love in our nature justice would never be born. For I do not call that justice which consists only in a sense of *our own* rights. True, there are poor and withered forms of love which are immeasurably below justice now; but even now they are of speechless worth, for they will grow into that which will supersede, because it will necessitate, Justice.

Of what use then is the law? To lead us to Christ, the Truth, – to waken in our minds a sense of what our deepest nature, the presence, namely, of God *in* us, requires of us, – to let us know, in part by failure, that the purest effort of will of which we are capable cannot lift us up even to the abstaining from wrong to our neighbour .... In order to fulfil the commonest law, I repeat, we must rise into a loftier region altogether, a region that is above law, because it is spirit and life and makes the law: in order to keep the law towards our neighbour, we must love our neighbour. We are not made for law, but for grace – or for faith, to use another word so much misused .... The laws comes to make us long for the needful grace, that is, for the divine condition, in which love is all, for God is Love ....

Thou shalt love thy neighbour as thyself ....

'But how,' says a man, who is willing to recognize the universal neighbourhead, but finds himself unable to fulfil the bare law towards the woman even who he loves best, – 'How am I then to rise into that higher region, that empyrean of love?' And beginning straightway to try to love his neighbour he finds that the empyrean of which he spoke is no more to be reached in itself than the law was to be reached in itself. As he cannot keep the law without first rising into the love of his neighbour, so he cannot love his neighbour without first rising higher still. The whole system of the universe works upon this law – the driving of things upward towards the centre. The man who will love his neighbour can do so by no immediately operative exercise of the will. It is the man fulfilled of God from whom he came and by whom he is, who alone can as himself love his neighbour who came from God too and is by God too. The mystery of individuality and consequent relation is deep as the beginnings of humanity, and the questions thence arising can be solved only by him who has, practically, at least, solved the holy necessities resulting from his origin. In God alone can man meet man. In him alone the converging lines of existence touch and cross not. When the mind of Christ, the life of the Head, courses through that atom which the man is of the slowly revivifying body, when he is alive too, then the love of the brothers is there as conscious life. From Christ through the neighbours comes the life that makes him a part of the body.

It *is* possible to love our neighbour as ourselves. Our Lord *never* spoke hyperbolically, although, indeed, that is the supposition on which many unconsciously interpret his words, in order to be able to persuade themselves that they believe them. We may see that it is possible before we attain to it; for our perceptions of truth are always in advance of our condition. True, no man can see it perfectly until he is it; but we must see it, that we may be it. A man who knows that he does not yet love his neighbour as himself may believe in such a condition, may even see that there is no other goal of human perfection, nothing else to which the universe is speeding, propelled by the Father's will. Let him labour on, and not faint at the thought that God's day is a thousand years: his millennium is likewise one day – yea, this day, for we have him, The Love, in us, working even now the far end.[37]

NEARER TO GOD
THAN IN OUR HUMAN RELATIONS

Reflections on Jesus' response to his mother and kinsmen when they
called for him to leave the crowds he had been teaching
(Matthew 12: 50).

But was he putting away his mother? Was it an unkind, an unfilial
thing to say? Did he, in saying, 'Who is my mother, who is my
brother?' repudiate the earthly mother and the earthly brother
and sister? No, verily. But, friends, it is a profound, absolute fact
that our relation to God is infinitely nearer than any relation by
nature. Our mother does not make us; we come forth of her but
forth also of the very soul of God. We are nearer, unspeakably nearer,
infinitely and unintelligibly (to our very poor intellects) nearer to
God than to the best, loveliest, dearest mother on the face of the
earth. The Lord, first of all, only spake an absolute fact; but then he
goes deeper and deeper still. This cannot be until the thing is known
and acknowledged. But look: if a mother has two children, one of
whom is as bad as a boy can be, and the other as good; the one is her
child and the other is not her child; they are both born of her body,
but the one that loves her and obeys her is born of her soul; yea, of
her very spirit, and she says, 'This is my child', and she says to the
other, with groans, 'You are none of mine'. And his being no child
is the misery of the thing; she would die for the one who is no child,
but for the one who is her child she would live forever.

And so when we become the sons and daughters of God indeed
by saying, 'Oh, my Father, I care for nothing but what thou carest
for; I will not lament for this thing; because I see thou dost not
care about it, I will not care either'; when you say, 'This is sore to bear,
but it is thy will, and therefore I thank thee for it, so sure am I of thy
will, O my Father in heaven': when we come to be able to talk like
that, then we are in the same mind as Jesus Christ whose delight, and
whose only delight, was to do the will of his Father in heaven. But
for God's sake, do not cling to your own poor will. It is not worth
having. It is a poor, miserable, degrading thing to fall down and
worship the inclination of your own heart, which may have come

from any devil, or from any accident of your birth, or from the weather, or from anything. Take the will of God, eternal, pure, strong, living, and true, the only good thing take that, and Christ will be your brother. If we knew the glory of that, I believe we could even delight in going against the poor small things that we should like in ourselves, delight even in thwarting ourselves.

To return to my subject. Was Christ refusing his mother? Was he saying, 'I come of another breed, and I have nothing to do with you?' Was that the spirit of it? The Son of God forbid! Never, never! But I must show here a deeper and a better thing. It is of the wisdom and tenderness of God that we come into the world as we do that we form families, little centres, and groups of spiritual nerves and power in the world. I do not see how in any other way we come to understand God. And, oh! you parents, who make it impossible for your children to understand God, what shall be said of or for you? If we had not fathers and mothers to love, I do not know how our hearts would understand God at all. I know not how I ever should. Then, again, if we had no brothers and sisters to love, how ever should we begin to learn this essential thing, that we should love our neighbour – that is, every man who comes near us to be affected with look or word – as ourselves? It were an impossibility. God begins with us graciously and easily. He brings us near, first, to mother, then to father, then to sister, then to brother – brings us so near to them that we cannot escape them. The months of infancy and the years of childhood are unspeakably precious from this fact, that we cannot escape the holy influences of family. So many are our needs, so quiescent are our needs, that love is, as it were, heaped upon us and forced into us: and we are taught – as we cannot help learning – to love.

But woe to the man or woman who stops there, and can only love because the child, or the sister, or the brother is his or hers! The same human soul, the same hungry human affection, the same aspiring, although blotted and spoiled, human spirit, is within every head, dwelling in every heart, and we are brothers and sisters wherever God has made man or woman, and until we have learned that, we are only going on, it may be a little, to learn Christ, but we have not yet learned him. What! Shall Christ love a man, and I not love him? Shall Christ say to a woman, 'My sister', and I not bow before her! It is preposterous. But then my own mother, my own father, my own brothers and sisters – if they be his too, they come first, they come nearer. But I do assert that there is a closer, infinitely closer, relation between any one that loves God and any other that loves God, than there is between any child and any mother where they do not both love him. The one has its root, the other has its leaves and flowers as well. We cannot love anybody too much; but we do not, we can never, love our own child aright until we have learned to love – not the mildness of the child – but the humanity of the child, the goodness, the thing that God meant, that came out of his will. That is the thing we have to love even in our children, or else the love is a poor dying thing, because we ourselves are dying. I am supposing that we do not possess the love of God, which is the only eternal thing. But if we love God, dearer and dearer grow the faces of father and mother, wife and child, until there is no end to it. It goes on, not only eternally in time, but eternally in growth, expanding. We do not understand it, because we are no farther on. Every bit we get farther, we understand more, and perceive more, and feel more; and the child of God is infinite, because he is a child of God. The child is like the Father. We have our share in God's infinitude, and therefore the Lord Christ himself called us 'gods' when he quoted from the Psalms. Whoever can, let him understand the words, 'I say, ye are gods'. The children of God must be gods in some sense. Little gods, indeed, but what is their completion and salvation? 'Ye shall sit down with me in my throne, even as I am set down with my Father in his throne.' And brothers and sisters, I cannot conceive any other sufficing redemption than this, that we should be set down on the throne of the King of kings, with the Lord our Master, as he said. Do you call this presumption? I appeal to Christ, for he has spoken. I believe in nothing but Christ; and so I trust to believe everything that is true, to know it when I see it.[38]

LOVING THE ENEMY

MacDonald comments on Jesus' command –
Love your enemies, bless them that curse you, do good them them that hate you,
and pray for them which despitefully use you, and persecute you:
that you may be the children of your Father which is in heaven ....
(Matthew 5: 43-48)

Is not this at length *too* much to expect? Will a man ever love his enemies? He may come to do good to them that hate him; but when will he pray for them that despitefully use him and persecute him? When? When he is the child of his Father in heaven. Then shall he love his neighbour as himself, even if that neighbour be his enemy. In the passage in Leviticus [19: 18] already referred to as quoted by our Lord and his apostles, we find the neighbour and the enemy are one. 'Thou shalt not avenge, nor bear any grudge against the children of thy people, but thou shalt love thy neighbour as thyself: I am the Lord.'

Look at the glorious way in which Jesus interprets the scripture that went before him. '*I am the Lord,* – That ye may be perfect, as your Father in heaven is perfect.' Is it then reasonable to love our enemies? God does; therefore it must be the highest reason. But is it reasonable to expect that man should become capable of doing so? Yes; on one ground: that the divine energy is at work in man, to render at length man's doing divine as his nature is. For this our Lord prayed when he said: 'That they all may be one as thou, Father, art in me, and I in thee, that they also may be one in us.' Nothing could be less likely to human judgment: our Lord knows that one day it will come.

Why should we love our enemies? The deepest reason for this we cannot put in words, for it lies in the absolute reality of their being, where our enemies are of one nature with us, even of the divine nature. Into this we cannot see, save as into a dark abyss. But we can adumbrate something of the form of this deepest reason, if we let the thoughts of our heart move upon the face of the dim profound.

'Are our enemies men like ourselves?' let me begin by asking. 'Yes.' 'Upon what ground? The ground of their enmity? The ground of the wrong they do us?' 'No.' 'In virtue of cruelty, heartlessness, injustice, disrespect, misrepresentation?' Certainly not, *Humanum est errare* is a truism; but it possesses, like most truisms, a latent germ of worthy truth. The very word *errare* is a sign that there is a way so truly the human that, for a man to leave it, is to *wander*. If it be human to wander, yet the wandering is not humanity. The very words *humane* and *humanity* denote some shadow of that loving-kindness which, when perfected after the divine fashion, shall include even our enemies. We do not call the offering of human sacrifices, the torturing of captives, cannibalism – humanity. Not because they do such deeds are they men. The humanity must be deeper than those. It is in virtue of the divine essence which is in them, that pure essential humanity, that we call our enemies men and women. It is this humanity that we are to love – a something, I say, deeper altogether than and independent of the region of hate. It is the humanity that originates the claim of neighbourhead; the neighbourhood only determines the occasion of its exercise. 'Is this humanity in every one of our enemies? 'Else there were nothing *to* love.' 'Is it there in very deed? – Then we *must* love it, come between us and it what may.'

But how can we love a man or a woman who is cruel and unjust to us? – who sears with contempt, or cuts with wrong every tendril we would put forth to embrace – who is mean, unlovely, carping, uncertain, self-righteous, self-seeking, and self-admiring? – who can even sneer, the most inhuman of human faults, far worse in its essence than mere murder?

These things cannot be loved. The best man hates them most; the worst man cannot love them. But are these the man? Does a woman bear that form in virtue of these? Lies there not within the man and the woman a divine element of brotherhood, of sisterhood, a something lovely and lovable, – slowly fading, it may be, dying away under the fierce heat of vile passions, or the yet more fearful cold of sepulchral selfishness – but there? Shall that divine something, which, once awakened to be its own holy self in the man, will loathe these unlovely things tenfold more than we loathe them now – shall this divine thing have no recognition from us? It is the very presence of this fading humanity that makes it possible for us to hate. If it were an animal only, and not a man or a woman that did us hurt, we should not hate; we should only kill. We hate the man just because we are prevented from loving him. We push over the verge of the creation – *we damn* – just because we cannot embrace. For to embrace is the necessity of our deepest being. That foiled, we hate. Instead of admonishing ourselves that there is our enchained brother, that there lies our enchanted, disfigured, scarce recognizable sister, captive of the devil, to break, how much sooner, from their bonds, that we love them! – we recoil into the hate which would fix them there; and the dearly lovable reality of them we sacrifice to the outer falsehood of Satan's incantations, thus leaving them to perish. Nay, we murder them to get rid of them. We *hate* them. Yet within the most obnoxious to our hate, lies that which, could it but show itself as it is, and as it will show itself one day, would compel from our hearts a devotion of love. It is not the unfriendly, the unlovely, that we are told to love, but the brother, the sister, who is unkind , who is unlovely. Shall we leave our brother to his desolate fate? Shall we not rather say, 'With my love at last shalt thou be compassed about, for thou hast not thy own lovingness to infold thee; love shall come as near thee as it may; and when thine comes forth to meet mine, we shall be one in the indwelling God'?

Let no one say I have been speaking in a figure merely. That I have been so speaking I know. But many things which we see most vividly and certainly are more truly expressed by using a right figure, than by attempting to give them a clear outline of logical expression. My figure means a truth.

If any one say, 'Do not make such vague distinctions. There is the person. Can you deny that that person is unlovely? How then can you love him?' I answer, 'That person, with the evil thing cast out of him, will be yet more the *person,* for he will be his real self. The thing that now makes you dislike him is separable from him, is therefore not he, makes himself so much less himself, for it is working death in him. Now he is in danger of ceasing to be a person at all. When he is clothed and in his right mind, he will be a person indeed. You *could* not then go on hating him. Begin to love him now, and help him into the loveliness which is his. Do not hate him although you can. The personality, I say, though clouded, besmeared, defiled with the wrong, lies deeper than the wrong, and indeed, so far as the wrong has reached it, is by the wrong injured, yea, so far, it may be, destroyed.[39]

BEING AND BELONGING TOGETHER

'Papa,' I said, 'why did you say we have done a wrong? You did not do it.'

'My dear boy, persons who are so near each other as we are, must not only bear the consequences together of any wrong done by one of them, but must, in a sense, bear each other's iniquities even. If I sin, you must suffer; if you sin, you being my own boy, I must suffer. But this is not all: it lies upon both of us to do what we can to get rid of the wrong done; and thus we have to bear each other's sin. I am accountable to make amends as far as I can; and also to do what I can to get you to be sorry and make amends as far as you can.'

'But, papa, isn't that hard?' I asked.

'Do you think I should like to leave you to get out of your sin as you best could, or sink deeper and deeper into it? Should I grudge anything to take the weight of the sin, or the wrong to others, off you?

'Do you think I should want not to be troubled about it? Or if I were to do anything wrong, would you think it very hard that you had to help me to be good, and set things right? Even if people looked down upon you because of me, would you say it was hard? Would you not rather say, "I'm glad to bear anything for my father: I'll share with him"?'

'Yes, indeed, papa. I would rather share with you than not, whatever it was.'

'Then you see, my boy, how kind God is in tying us up in one bundle that way. It is a grand and beautiful thing that the fathers should suffer for the children, and the children for the fathers. Come along. We must step out, or I fear we shall not be able to make our apology to-night. When we've got over this, Ranald, we must be a good deal more careful what company we keep.'[40]

Ever-widening Love

Narrator speaking of Marion.

Her society did much to keep my heart open and to prevent it from becoming selfishly absorbed in its cares for husband and children. For love which is *only* concentrating its force, that is, which is not at the same time widening its circle, is itself doomed, and for its objects ruinous, be those objects ever so sacred. God himself could never be content that his children should love him only; nor has he allowed the few to succeed who have tried after it: perhaps their divinest success has been their most mortifying failure. Indeed, for exclusive love, sharp suffering is often sent as the needful cure – needful to break the stony crust which, in the name of love for one's own, gathers about the divinely glowing core – a crust which, promising to cherish by keeping in the heat, would yet gradually thicken until all was crust; for truly, in things of the heart and spirit, as the warmth ceases to spread, the molten mass within ceases to glow, until at length, but for the divine care and discipline, there would be no love left for even spouse or child – only for self – which is eternal death.[41]

Relations are Symbols of Deeper Ties

I have wondered whether, if my father had lived to bring me up instead of my uncle, I should have been very different; but the useless speculation has only driven me to believe that the relations on the surface of life are but the symbols of far deeper ties, which may exist without those correspondent external ones. At the same time, now that, being old, I naturally think of the coming change, I feel that, when I see my father, I shall have a different feeling for him just because he is my father, although my uncle did all the fatherly toward me. But we need not trouble ourselves about our hearts, and all their varying hues and shades of feeling. Truth is at the root of all existence, therefore everything must come right if only we are obedient to the truth; and right is the deepest satisfaction of every creature as well as of God. I wait in confidence. If things be not as we think, they will both arouse and satisfy a better *think,* making us glad they are not as we expected.[42]

(8) *Living out Our Communion with Jesus Christ*

BECOMING THE IMAGE OF THE CHARACTER OF JESUS CHRIST

Commenting on II Corinthians 3: 18.

It seems, then, to me, that the true simple word to represent the Greek, and the most literal as well by which to translate it, is the verb *mirror* – when the sentence, so far, would run thus: 'But we all, with unveiled face, mirroring the glory of the Lord.'

I must now go on to unfold the idea at work in the heart of the apostle .... The prophet-apostle seems to me, then, to say, 'We all, with clear vision of the Lord, mirroring in our hearts his glory, even as a mirror would take into itself his face, are thereby changed into his likeness, his glory working our glory, by the present power, in our inmost being, of the Lord, the spirit.' Our mirroring of Christ, then, is one with the presence of his spirit in us. The idea, you see, is not the reflection, the radiating of the light of Christ on others, though that were a figure lawful enough; but the taking into, and having in us, him working to the changing of us.

That the thing signified transcends the sign, outreaches the figure, is no discovery; the thing figured always belongs to a higher stratum, to which the simile serves but as a ladder; when the climber has reached it, 'he then unto the ladder turns his back'. It is but according to the law of symbol, that the thing symbolized by the mirror could have properties far beyond those of leaded glass or polished metal, seeing it is a live soul understanding that which it takes into its deeps holding it, and conscious of what it holds. It mirrors by its will to hold in its mirror. Unlike symbol, it can hold not merely the outward usual resemblance, but the inward likeness of the person revealed by it; it is open to the influences of that which it embraces, and is capable of active co-operation with them: the mirror and the thing mirrored are of one origin and nature, and in closest relation to each other. Paul's idea is, that when we take into our understanding, our heart, our conscience, our being, the glory of God, namely Jesus Christ as he shows himself to our eyes, our hearts, our consciences, he works upon us, and will keep working, till we are changed to the very likeness we have thus mirrored in us; for with his likeness he comes himself, and dwells in us. He will work until the same likeness is wrought out and perfected in us, the image, namely, of the humanity of God, in which image we were made at first, but which could never be developed in us except by the indwelling of the perfect likeness. By the power of Christ thus received and at home in us, we are changed – the glory in him becoming glory in us, his glory changing us to glory.

But we must beware of receiving this or any symbol *after the flesh,* beware of interpreting it in any fashion that partakes of the character of the mere physical, psychical, or spirituo-mechanical. The symbol deals with things far beyond the deepest region whence symbols can be drawn. The indwelling of Jesus in the soul of man, who shall declare! But let us note this, that the dwelling of Jesus in us is the power of the spirit of God upon us; for 'the Lord is that spirit', and that Lord dwelling in us, we are changed 'even as from the Lord the spirit'. When we think Christ, Christ comes; when we receive his image into our spiritual mirror, he enters with it. Our thought is not cut off from his. Our open receiving thought is his door to come in. When our hearts turn to him, that is opening the door to him, that is holding up our mirror to him: then he comes in, not by our thought only, not in our idea only, but he comes himself, and of his own will – comes in as we could not take him, but as he can come and we receive him – enabled to receive by his very coming the one welcome guest of the whole universe. Thus the Lord, the spirit, becomes the soul of our souls, becomes spiritually what he always was creatively; and as our spirit informs, gives shape to our bodies, in like manner his soul informs, gives shape to our souls. In this there is nothing unnatural, nothing at conflict with our being. It is but that the deeper soul that willed and wills our souls, rises up, the infinite Life, into the Self we call *I* and *me*, but which lives immediately from him, and is his very own property and nature – unspeakably more his than ours: this deeper creative soul, working on and with his creation upon higher levels, makes the *I* and *me* more and more his, and himself more and more ours; until at length the glory of our existence flashes upon us, we face full to the sun that enlightens what it sent forth, and know ourselves alive with an infinite life, even the life of the Father; know that our existence is not the moonlight of a mere consciousness of being, but the sun-glory of a life justified by having become one with its origin, thinking and feeling with the primal Sun of life, from whom it was dropped away that it might know and bethink itself, and return to circle for ever in exultant harmony around him. Then indeed we *are;* then indeed we have life; the life of Jesus has, through light, become life in us; the glory of God in the face of Jesus, mirrored in our hearts, has made us alive; we are one with God for ever and ever.[43]

DENYING SELF FOR JOY

There is no joy belonging to human nature, as God made it, that shall not be enhanced a hundredfold to the man who gives up himself – though, in so doing, he may seem to be yielding the very essence of life. To yield self is to give up grasping at things in their second causes, as men call them, but which are merely God's means, and to receive them direct from their source – to take them seeing whence they come, and not as if they came from nowhere, because no one appears presenting them. The careless soul receives the Father's gifts as if it were a way things had of dropping into his hand. He thus grants himself a slave, dependent on chance and his own blundering endeavour – yet is he ever complaining, as if some one were accountable for the checks which meet him at every turn. For the good that comes to him, he gives no thanks – who is there to thank? at the disappointments that befall him he grumbles – there must be some one to blame! He does not think to what Power it could be of any consequence, nay, what power would not be worse than squandered, to sustain him after his own fashion, in his paltry, low-aimed existence! How could a God pour out his being to uphold the merest waste of his creatures? No world could ever be built or sustained on such an idea. It is the children who shall inherit the earth; such as will not be children, cannot possess. The hour is coming when all that art, all that science, all that nature, all that animal nature, in ennobling subjugation to the higher even as man is subject to the Father, can afford, shall be the possession, to the endless delight, of the sons and daughters of God: to him to whom he is all in all, God is able to give these things; to another he cannot give them, for he is unable to receive them who [are] outside the truth of them. Assuredly we are not to love God for the sake of what he can give us; nay, it is impossible to love him save because he is our God, and altogether good and beautiful; but neither may we forget what the Lord does not forget, that, in the end, when the truth is victorious God will answer his creature in the joy of his heart. For what is joy but the harmony of the spirit! The good Father made his children to be joyful; only, ere they can enter into his joy, they must be like himself, ready to sacrifice joy to truth. No promise of such joy is an appeal to selfishness. Every reward held out by Christ is a pure thing; nor can it enter the soul save as a death to selfishness. The heaven of Christ is a loving of all, a forgetting of self, a dwelling of each in all, and all in each. Even in our nurseries, a joyful child is rarely selfish, generally righteous. It is not selfish to be joyful .... It may be deep selfishness to refuse to be happy.[44]

THE GOD WHO HEARS US

The impossibility of doing what we would as we would, drives us to look for help. And this brings us to a new point of departure. Every thing difficult indicates something more than our theory of life yet embraces, checks some tendency to abandon the strait path, leaving open only the way ahead. But there is a reality of being in which all things are easy and plain – oneness, that is, with the Lord of Life; to pray for this is the first thing; and to the point of this prayer every

difficulty hedges and directs us. But if I try to set forth something
of the reasonableness of all prayer, I beg my readers to remember
that it is for the sake of action and not speculation; if prayer be
anything at all, it is a thing to be done: what matter whether you
agree with me or not, if you do not pray? I would not spend my
labour for that; I desire it to serve for help to pray, not to understand
how a man might pray and yet be a reasonable soul ....

* * *

Concerning the parable of the woman
who perseveres with her request to a judge – (Luke 18: 1-8).

Here then is a word of the Lord about prayer: it is a comfort that he
recognizes difficulty in the matter – sees that we need encouragement
to go on praying, that it looks as if we were not heard, that it is no
wonder we should be ready to faint and leave off. He tells a parable
in which the suppliant has to go often and often to the man who can
help her, gaining her end only at the long last. Actual delay on the
part of God, we know from what follows, he does not allow; the
more plain is it that he recognizes how the thing must look to those
whom he would have go on praying. Here as elsewhere he teaches us
that we must not go by the look of things, but by the reality behind
the look. A truth, a necessity of God's own willed nature, is enough
to set up against a whole army of appearances. It looks as if he did
not hear you: never mind; he does; it must be that he does; go on as
the woman did; you too will be heard. She is heard at last, and in
virtue of her much going; God hears at once, and will avenge speedily. The unrighteous judge cared nothing for the woman; those who
cry to God are his own chosen – plain in the fact that they cry to him.
He has made and appointed them to cry: they do cry: will he not hear
them? They exist that they may pray; he has chosen them that they
may choose him; he has called them that they may call him – that
there may be such communion such interchange as belongs to their
being and the being of their Father. The gulf of indifference lay
between the poor woman and the unjust judge; God and those who
seek his help, are closer than two hands clasped hard in love: he

will avenge them speedily. It is a bold assertion in the face of what
seems great delay – an appearance acknowledged in the very ground-
work of the parable.[45]

GIVER AND GIFT

'But if God is so good as you represent him, and if he knows all
that we need, and better far than we do ourselves, why should it
be necessary to ask him for anything?'

I answer, What if he knows prayer to be the thing we need first
and most? What if the main object in God's idea of prayer be the
supplying of our great, our endless need – the need of himself?
What if the good of all our smaller and lower needs lies in this,
that they help to drive us to God? Hunger may drive the runaway
child home, and he may or may not be fed at once, but he needs
his mother more than his dinner. Communion with God is the one
need of the soul beyond all other need; prayer is the beginning of
that communion, and some need is the motive of that prayer. Our
wants are for the sake of our coming into communion with God, our
eternal need. If gratitude and love immediately followed the supply
of our needs, if God our Saviour was the one thought of our hearts,
then it might be unnecessary, that we should ask for anything we
need. But seeing we take our supplies as a matter of course, feeling
as if they came out of nothing, or from the earth, or our own
thoughts, instead of out of a heart of love and a will which alone is
force, it is needful that we should be made feel some at least our
wants, that we may seek him who alone supplies all of them, and find
his every gift a window to his heart of truth. So begins a communion,
a talking with God, a coming-to-one with him, which is the sole end
of prayer, yea, of existence itself in its infinite phases. We must ask
that we may receive; but that we should receive what we ask in
respect of our lower needs, is not God's end in making us pray, for
he could give us everything without that: to bring his child to his
knee, God withholds that man may ask.

In regard, however, to the high necessities of our nature, it is
in order that he may be able to give that God requires us to ask –

requires by driving us to it – by shutting us up to prayer. For how can he give into the soul of a man what it needs, while that soul cannot receive it? The ripeness for receiving is the asking. The blossom-cup of the soul, to be filled with the heavenly dews, is its prayer. When the soul is hungry for the light, for the truth – when its hunger has waked its higher energies, thoroughly roused the will, and brought the soul into its highest condition, that of action, its only fitness for receiving the things of God, that action is prayer. Then God can give; then he can be as he would towards the man; for the glory of God is to give himself. – We thank thee, Lord Christ, for by thy pain alone do we rise towards the knowledge of this glory of thy Father and our Father.

And even in regard to lower things – what it may be altogether unfit to do for a man who does not recognize the source of his life, it may be in the highest sense fit to grant him when he comes to that source to ask for it. Even in the case of some individual desire of one who in the main recognizes the Father, it may be well to give him asking whom, not asking, it would not benefit. For the real good of every gift it is essential, first, that the giver be in the gift – as God always is, for he is love – and next, that the receiver know and receive the giver in the gift. Every gift of God is but a harbinger of his greatest and only sufficing gift – that of himself. No gift un-recognized as coming from God is at its own best; therefore many things that God would gladly give us, things even that we need because we are, must wait until we ask for them, that we may know whence they come: when in all gifts we find him, then in him we shall find all things.[46]

BLESSED ARE THOSE WHO MOURN

A reflection on the beatitude in Matthew 5: 4 –
Blessed are they that mourn, for they shall be comforted.

Grief, then, sorrow, pain of heart, mourning, is no partition-wall between man and God. So far is it from opposing any obstacle to the passage of God's light into man's soul, that the Lord congratulates them that mourn. There is no evil in sorrow. True, it is not an essential good, a good in itself, like love; but it will mingle with any good thing, and is even so allied to good that it will open the door of the heart for any good. More of sorrowful than of joyful men are always standing about the everlasting doors that open into the presence of the Most High. It is true also that joy is in its nature more divine than sorrow; for, although man must sorrow, and God share in his sorrow, yet in himself God is not sorrowful, and the 'glad creator' never made man for sorrow: it is but a stormy strait through which he must pass to his ocean of peace. He 'makes the joy the last in every song'. Still, I repeat, a man in sorrow is in general far nearer God than a man in joy. Gladness may make a man forget his thanksgiving; misery drives him to his prayers. For we *are* not yet, we are only *becoming*. The endless day will at length dawn whose every throbbing moment will heave our hearts Godward; we shall scarce need to lift them up: now, there are two door-keepers to the house of prayer, and Sorrow is more on the alert to open than her grandson Joy.

The gladsome child runs farther afield; the wounded child turns to go home. The weeper sits down close to the gate; the lord of life draws nigh to him from within. God loves not the sorrow, yet rejoices to see a man sorrowful, for in his sorrow man leaves his heavenward door on the latch, and God can enter to help him. He loves, I say, to see him sorrowful, for then he can come near to part him from that which makes his sorrow a welcome sight.

When Ephraim bemoans himself, he is a pleasant child. So good a medicine is sorrow, so powerful to slay the moths of infest and devour the human heart, that the Lord is glad to see a man weep. He congratulates him on his sadness. Grief is an ill-favoured thing, but she is Love's own child, and her mother loves her.

The promise to them that mourn, is not the *kingdom of heaven*, but that their mourning shall be ended, that they shall be comforted. To mourn is not to fight with evil; it is only to miss that which is good. It is not an essential heavenly condition, like poorness of spirit or meekness. No man will carry his mourning with him into heaven – or, if he does, it will speedily be turned either into joy, or into what will result in joy, namely, redemptive action.

Mourning is a canker-bitten blossom on the rosetree of love. Is there any mourning worthy the name that has not love for its root? Men mourn because they love. Love is the life out of which are fashioned all the natural feelings, every emotion of man. Love modelled by faith, is hope; love shaped by wrong, is anger – verily anger, though pure of sin; love invaded by loss, is grief.

The garment of mourning is oftenest a winding-sheet; the loss of the loved by death is the main cause of the mourning of the world. The Greek word here used to describe the blessed of the Lord, generally means *those that mourn for the dead.* It is not in the New Testament employed exclusively in this sense, neither do I imagine it stands here for such only: there are griefs than death sorer far, and harder far to comfort – harder even for God himself, with whom all things are possible; but it may give pleasure to know that the promise of comfort to those that mourn, may specially apply to those that mourn, because their loved have gone out of their sight, and beyond the reach of their cry. Their sorrow, indeed, to the love divine, involves no difficulty; it is a small matter, easily met. The father, whose elder son is ever with him, but whose younger is in a far country, wasting his substance with riotous living, is unspeakably more to be pitied, and is harder to help, than that father both of whose sons lie in the sleep of death.[47]

TRUE SERVICE

Do not forget the true notion of service as the essence of Christianity, yea, for divinity. It is not education that unfits for service; it is the want of it ...

Not one of the maids to whom you have referred had ever been taught to think service other than an unavoidable necessity, the end of life being to serve yourself, not to serve others .... The only way to set them free is to get them to regard service not only as their duty, but as therefore honourable, and besides and beyond this, in its own nature divine .... There is no dignity but of service. How different the whole notion of training is now from what it was in the middle ages! Service was honourable then. No doubt we have made progress as a whole, but in some things we have degenerated sadly.

The first thing taught then was how to serve. No man could rise to the honour of knighthood without service. A nobleman's son even had to wait on his father, or to go into the family of another nobleman, and wait upon him as a page, standing behind his chair at dinner. This was an honour. No notion of degradation was in it. It was a necessary step to higher honour. And what was the next higher honour? To be set free from service? No. To serve in the harder service of the field; to be a squire to some noble knight; to tend his horse, to clean his armour, to see that every rivet was sound, every buckle true, every strap strong; to ride behind him and carry his spear, and if more than one attacked him, to rush to his aid. This service was the more honourable because it was harder, and was the next step to higher honour yet. And what was this higher honour? That of knighthood. Wherein did this knighthood consist? The very word means simply service. And for what was the knight thus waited upon by his squire? That he might be free to do as he pleased? No, but that he might be free to be the servant of all. By being a squire first, the servant of one, he learned to rise to the higher rank, that of servant of all. His horse was tended, his armour observed, his sword and spear and shield held to his hand, that he might have no trouble looking after himself, but might be free, strong, unwearied, to shoot like an arrow to the rescue of any and every one who needed his ready aid. There was a grand heart of Christianity in that old chivalry, notwithstanding all its abuses ... [it was] the lack of it, not the presence of it, that occasioned the abuses that co-existed with it.[48]

ALL TO THE GLORY

Mr Drew, a draper, is a member of Thomas Wingfold's congregation.
Mr Drew is recounting his reflections since the sermon
he heard Wingfold preach the previous Sunday.

'Now, whether it was anything you had said coming back to me I cannot tell, but next day, that was yesterday, all at once, in the shop here, as I was serving Mrs Ramshorn, the thought came to me, How would Jesus Christ have done if he had been a draper instead of a carpenter? When she was gone, I went up to my room to think about it. And there it seemed that first I must know how he did as a carpenter. But that we are told nothing about. I could get no light upon that. And so my thoughts turned again to the original question, How would he have done had he been a draper? And, strange to say, I seemed to know far more about that than the other, and to have something to go upon. In fact, I had a sharp and decisive answer concerning several things of which I had dared to make a question.'

'The vision of the ideal woke the ideal in yourself,' said Wingfold thoughtfully.

'I don't know that I quite understand that,' returned Mr. Drew; 'but the more I thought the more dissatisfied I became. And, in a word, it has come to this, that I must set things right or give up business.'

'That would be no victory,' remarked the curate.

'I know it, and shall not yield without a struggle, I promise you. That same afternoon, taking the opportunity of having overheard one of them endeavouring to persuade an old farmer's wife to her disadvantage, I called all my people, and told them that if ever I heard one of them do such a thing, I would turn him or her away at once. But when I came to look at it, I saw how difficult it would be to convict of the breach of such a vague law; and unfortunately, too, I had some time ago introduced the system of a small percentage to the sellers, making it their interest to force sales. That, however, is easily rectified, and I shall see to it at once. But I do wish I had a more definite law to follow than that of doing as!'

'Would not more light inside do as well as clearer law outside?' suggested Wingfold.

'How can I tell till I have had a chance of trying?' returned the draper with a smile, which speedily vanished as he went on: 'Then, again, there's all about profits! How much ought I to take? Am I to do as others do, and always be ruled by the market? Am I bound to give my customers the advantage of any special bargain I may have made? And then again – for I do a large wholesale business with the little country shops – if I learn that one of my customers is going down-hill, have I or have I not a right to pounce upon him and make him pay me, to the detriment of his other creditors? There's no end of questions, you see, sir.'

'I am the worst possible man to ask,' returned Wingfold again. 'I might, from very ignorance, judge that wrong which is really right, or that right which is really wrong. But one thing I begin to see, that before a man can do right by his neighbour, he must love him as himself. Only I am such a poor scholar in these high things that, as you have just said, I cannot pretend to teach anybody. That sermon was but an appeal to men's own consciences whether they kept the words of the Lord by whose name they called themselves. Except in your case, Mr Drew, I am not aware that one of the congregation has taken it to heart.'

'I am not sure of that,' returned the draper. 'Some talk among my own people has made me fancy that, perhaps, though talk be but froth, the froth may rise from some hot work down below. Never man could tell from the quiet way I am talking to you how much I have felt in these few days past.'

Wingfold looked him in the face: the earnestness of the man was plain in his eyes, and his resolve stamped on every feature. The curate thought of Zacchaeus; thought of Matthew at the receipt of custom; thought with some shame of certain judgments concerning trade, and shopkeepers especially, that seemed somehow to have bred in him like creeping things; for whence they had come he could not tell.[49]

(9) *God's Good Creation in Christ*

THE HOPE FOR ALL CREATURES

Commenting on Romans 8: 19 –
For the earnest expectation of the creature
waiteth for the manifestation of the sons of God.

… In the term *creation,* Paul comprises all creatures capable of suffering; the condition of which sentient, therefore superior portion, gives him occasion to speak of the whole creation as suffering in the process of its divine evolution or development, groaning and travailing as in the pangs of giving birth to a better self, a nobler world. It is not necessary to the idea that the creation should know what it is groaning after, or wherein the higher condition constituting its deliverance must consist. The human race groans for deliverance: how much does the race know that its redemption lies in becoming one with the Father, and partaking of his glory? Here and there one of the race knows it – which is indeed a pledge for the race – but the race cannot be said to know its own lack, or to have even a far-off notion of what alone can stay its groaning. In like manner the whole creation is groaning after an unforeseen yet essential birth – groans with the necessity of being freed from a state that is but a transitional and not a true one, from a condition that nowise answers to the intent in which existence began. In both the lower creation and the higher, this same groaning of the fettered idea after a freer life, seems the first enforced decree of a holy fate, and itself the first movement of the hampered thing toward the liberty of another birth.

To believe that God made many of the lower creatures merely for prey, or to be the slaves of a slave, and writhe under the tyrannies of a cruel master who will not serve his own master; that he created and is creating an endless succession of them to reap little or no good of life but its cessation – a doctrine held by some, and practically accepted by multitudes – is to believe in a God who, so far as one portion at least of his creation is concerned, is a demon. But a creative demon is an absurdity; and were such a creator possible, he would not be God, but must one day be found and destroyed by the real God. Not the less the fact remains, that miserable suffering abounds among them, and that, even supposing God did not foresee how creation would turn out for them, the thing lies at his door. He has besides made them so far dumb that they cannot move the hearts of the oppressors into whose hands he has given them, telling how hard they find the world, how sore their life in it. The apostle takes up their case, and gives us material or an answer to such as blame God for their sad condition ....

What many men call their beliefs, are but the prejudices they happen to have picked up: why should such believers waste a thought as to how their paltry fellow-inhabitants of the planet fare? Many indeed have all their lives been too busy making their human fellows groan and sweat for their own fancied well-being, to spare a thought for the fate of the yet more helpless. But there are not a few, who would be indignant at having their belief in God questioned, who yet seem greatly to fear imagining him better than he is: whether is it he or themselves they dread injuring by expecting too much of him? 'You see the plain facts of the case!' they say. 'There is no questioning them! What can be done for the poor things – except indeed you take the absurd notion into your head, that they too have a life beyond the grave?'

Why should such a notion seem to you absurd? I answer. The teachers of the nation have unwittingly, it seems to me through unbelief, wronged the animals deeply by their silence, lament the thoughtless popular presumption that they have no hereafter; thus leaving them deprived of a great advantage to their position among men. But I suppose they too have taken it for granted that the Preserver of man and beast never had a thought of keeping one beast alive beyond a certain time; in which case heartless men might well argue he did not care how they wronged them, for he meant them no redress. Their immortality is no new faith with me, but as old as my childhood.

Do you believe in immortality for yourself? I would ask any reader who is not in sympathy with my hope for the animals. If not, I have no argument with you. But if you do, why not believe in it for them? Verily, were immortality no greater a thing for the animals than it seems for men to some who yet profess to expect it, I should scarce care to insist upon their share in it. But if the thought be anywise precious to you, is it essential to your enjoyment in it, that nothing less than yourself should share its realization? Are you the lowest kind of creature that *could* be permitted to live? Had God been of like heart with you, would he have given life and immortality to creatures so much less than himself as we? Are these not worth making immortal? How, then, were they worth calling out of the depth of no-being? It is a greater deed, to make be that which was not, than to seal it with an infinite immortality: did God do that which was not worth doing? What he thought worth making, you think not worth continuing made! You would have him go on for ever creating new things with one hand, and annihilating those he had made with the other – for I presume you would not prefer the earth to be without animals! If it were harder for God to make the former go on living, than to send forth new, then his creatures were no better than the toys which a child makes, and destroys as he makes them. For what good, for what divine purpose is the maker of the sparrow present at its death, if he does not care what becomes of it? What is he there for, I repeat, if he gave no care that it go well with his bird in its dying, that it be neither comfortless nor lost in the abyss? If his presence be no good to the sparrow, are you very sure what good it will be to you when your hour comes? Believe it is not by a little only that the heart the universe is tenderer, more loving, more just and fair, than yours or mine.

If you did not believe you were yourself to outlive death, I could not blame you for thinking all was over with the sparrow; but to believe in immortality for yourself, and not care to believe in it for the sparrow, would be simply hard-hearted and selfish. If it would make you happy to think there was life beyond death for the sparrow a well as for yourself, I would gladly help you at least to hope that there may be.

I know of no reason why I should not look for the animals to rise again, in the same sense in which I hope myself to rise again – which is, to reappear, clothed with another and better form of life than before. If the Father will raise his children, why should he not also raise those whom he has taught his little ones to love? Love is the one bond of the universe, the heart of God, the life of his children: if animals can be loved they are loveable; if they can love, they are yet more plainly loveable: love is eternal; how then should its object perish? Must the very immortality of love divide the bond of love? Must the love live on for ever without its object? or worse still, must the love die with its object, and be eternal no more than it? What a misinvented correlation in which the one side was eternal, the other, where not yet annihilated, constantly perishing! Is not our love to the animals a precious variety of love? And if God gave the creatures to us, that a new phase of love might be born in us toward another kind of life from the same fountain, why should the new life be more perishing than the new love? Can you imagine that, if, hereafter, one of God's little ones were to ask him to give again one of the earth's old loves – kitten, or pony, or squirrel, or dog, which he had taken from him, the Father would say no? If the thing was so good that God made it for and gave it to the child at first who never asked for it, why should he not give it again to the child who prays for it because the Father had made him love it? What a child may ask for, the Father will keep ready.

That there are difficulties in the way of believing thus, I grant; that there are impossibilities, I deny .... [50]

CREATION SIGNALS THE INCARNATE REVELATION

Commenting on a hymn concerning
the creation's display of the Creator's power.

Whether indeed the heavenly bodies teach what he says, or whether we should read divinity worthy of the name in them at all, without the human revelation which healed men, I doubt much. That divinity is there – *Yes;* that we could read it there without having seen the face of the Son of Man first, I think – *No.* I do not therefore dare imagine that no revelation dimly leading towards such result glimmered in the hearts of God's chosen amongst Jews and Gentiles before he came. What I say is, that power and order, although of God, and preparing the way for him, are not his revealers unto men. No doubt King David compares the perfection of God's law to the glory of the heavens, but he did not learn that perfection from the heavens, but from the law itself, revealed in his own heart through the life-teaching of God. When he had learned it he saw that the heavens were like it.

To unveil God, only manhood like our own will serve. And he has taken the form of man that he might reveal the manhood in him from awful eternity.[51]

The Deeper Meaning discerned in the Face of Nature

In what belongs to the deeper meanings of nature and her mediation between us and God, the appearances of nature are the truths of nature, far deeper than any scientific discoveries in and concerning them. The show of things is that for which God cares *most,* for their show is the face of far deeper things than they; we see in them, in a distant way, as in a glass darkly, the face of the unseen. It is through their show, not through their analysis, that we enter into their deepest truths. What they say to the childlike soul is the truest thing to be gathered of them. To know a primrose is a higher thing than to know all the botany of it – just as to know Christ is an infinitely higher thing than to know all theology, all that is said about His person, or babbled about His work. The body of man does not exist for the sake of its hidden secrets; its hidden secrets exist for the sake of its outside – for the face and the form in which dwells revelation: its outside is the deepest of it. So Nature as well exists primarily for her face, her look, her appeals to the heart and the imagination, her simple service to human need, and not for the secrets to be discovered in her and turned to man's further use.[52]

Children's Delights

For innocent animal delight, I know of nothing to match those days – so warm, yet so pure-aired – so clean, so glad. I often think how God must love his little children to have invented for them such delights! For, of course, if he did not love the children and delight in their pleasure, he would not have invented the two and brought them together. Yes, my child, I know what you would say, – 'How many there are who have no such pleasures!' I grant it sorrowfully; but you must remember that God has not done with them yet; and, besides, that there are more pleasures in the world than you or I know anything about. And if we had it *all* pleasure, I know I should not care so much about what is better, and I would rather be made good than have any other pleasure in the world; and so would you, though perhaps you do not know it yet.[53]

Meanings within Creation

No thought, human or divine, can be conveyed from man to man, save through the symbolism of the creation. The heavens and the earth are around us that it may be possible for us to speak of the unseen by the seen; for the outermost husk of creation has correspondence with the deepest things of the Creator. He is not a God that hideth himself, but a God who made that he might reveal; he is consistent and one throughout. There are things with which an enemy hath meddled; but there are more things with which no enemy could meddle, and by which we may speak of God. They may not have revealed him to us, but at least when he is revealed, they show themselves so much of his nature, that we at once use them as spiritual tokens in the commerce of the spirit, to help convey to other minds what we may have seen of the unseen.'[54]

Miracles and Creation

Here I will suppose some honest, and therefore honourable, reader objecting: But do you not thus place the miracles in dignity below the ordinary processes of nature? I answer: The miracles are mightier far than any goings on of nature as beheld by common eyes, dissociating them from a living Will; but the miracles are surely less than those mighty goings on of nature with God beheld at their heart. In the name of him who delighted to say 'My Father is greater than I', I will say that his miracles in bread and in wine were far less grand and less beautiful than the works of the Father they represented, in making the corn to grow in the valleys, and the grapes to drink the sunlight on the hill-sides of the world, with all their infinitudes of tender gradation and delicate mystery of birth. But the Son of the Father be praised, who, as it were, condensed these mysteries before us, and let us see the precious gifts coming at once from gracious hands – hands that love could kiss and nails could wound.

There are some, I think, who would perhaps find it more possible to accept the New Testament story if the miracles did not stand in the way. But perhaps, again, it would be easier for them to accept both if they could once look into the true heart of these miracles. So long as they regard only the surface of them, they will, most likely, see in them only a violation of the laws of nature: when they behold the heart of them, they will recognize there at least a possible fulfillment of her deepest laws. With such, however, is not my main business now, any more than with those who cannot believe in a God at all, and therefore to whom a miracle is an absurdity. I may, however, just make this one remark with respect to the latter – that perhaps it is better they should believe in no God than believe in such a God as they have yet been able to imagine. Perhaps thus they are nearer to a true faith – except indeed they prefer the notion of the Unconscious generating the Conscious, to that of a self-existent Love, creative in virtue of its being love. Such have never loved woman or child save after a fashion which has left them content that death should seize on the beloved and bear them back to the maternal dust. But I doubt if there can be any who thus would choose a sleep-walking Pan before a wakeful Father. At least, they cannot know the Father and choose the Pan.

Let us then recognize the works of the Father as epitomized in the miracles of the Son. What in the hands of the Father are the mighty motions and progresses and conquests of life, in the hands of the Son are miracles. I do not myself believe that he valued the working of these miracles as he valued the utterance of the truth in words; but all that he did had the one root, *obedience,* in which alone can any son be free. And what is the highest obedience? Simply a following of the Father – a doing of what the Father does. Every true father wills that his child should be as he is in his deepest love, in his highest hope. All that Jesus does is of his Father. What we see in the Son is of the Father. What his works mean concerning him, they mean concerning the Father.

Much as I shrink from the notion of a formal shaping out of design in any great life, so unlike the endless freedom and spontaneity of nature (and He is the Nature of nature), I cannot help observing that his first miracle [changing water to wine at the wedding in Cana] was one of creation – at least, is to our eyes more like creation than almost any other – for who can say that it was creation, not knowing in the least what creation is, or what was the process in this miracle?[55]

(10) *Our Eternal Hope and Inheritance*

HEAVEN'S BEYOND OUR WEAK IMAGININGS

Children fear heaven, because of the dismal notions the unchild-like give them of it, who, without imagination, receive unquestioning what others, as void of imagination as themselves, represent concerning it. I do not see that one should care to present an agreeable picture of it; for, suppose I could persuade a man that heaven was the perfection of all he could desire around him, what would the man or the truth gain by it? If he knows the Lord, he will not trouble himself about heaven; if he does not know him, he will not be drawn to *him* by it. I would not care to persuade the feeble Christian that heaven was a place worth going to; I would rather persuade him that no spot in space, no hour in eternity is worth anything to one who remains such as he is. But would that none presumed to teach the little ones what they know nothing of themselves! What have not children suffered from strong endeavour to desire the things they could not love! Well do I remember the pain of prospect – no, the trouble at not being pleased with the prospect – of being made a pillar in the house of God, and going no more out! Those words were not spoken to the little ones. Yet are they, literally taken, a blessed promise compared with the notion of a continuous church going! Perhaps no one teaches such a thing; but somehow the children get the dreary fancy: there are ways of involuntary teaching more potent than words. What boy, however fain to be a disciple of Christ and a child of God, would prefer a sermon to his glorious kite, that divinest of toys, with God himself for his playmate, in the blue wind that tossed it hither and thither in the golden void! He might be ready to part with kite and wind and sun, and go down to the grave for his brothers – but surely not that they might be admitted to an ever-lasting prayer-meeting! For my own part, I rejoice to think that there will be neither church nor chapel in the high countries; yea, that there will be nothing there called religion, and no law but the perfect law of liberty. For how should there be law or religion where every throb of the heart says *God!* where every songthroat is eager with thanksgiving where such a tumult of glad waters is for ever burst-ing from beneath the throne of God, the tears of the gladness of the universe! Religion? Where will be the room for it, when the essence of every thought must be God? Law? What room will there be for law, when everything upon which law could lay a *shalt not* will be too loathsome to think of? What room for honesty, where love fills full the law to overflowing – where a man would rather drop sheer into the abyss, than wrong his neighbour one hair's-breadth?

Heaven will be continuous touch with God. The very sense of being will in itself be bliss. For the sense of true life, there must be actual, conscious contact with the source of the life; therefore mere life – in itself, in its very essence good – good as the life of God which is our life – must be such bliss as, I think, will need the mit-igation of the loftiest joys of communion with our blessed fellows; the mitigation of art in every shape, and of all combinations of arts; the mitigation of countless services to the incomplete, and hard toil for those who do not yet know their neighbour or their Father. The bliss of pure being will, I say, need these mitigations to render the intensity of it endurable by heart and brain.

To those who care only for things, and not for the souls of them, for the truth, the reality of them, the prospect of inheriting light can have nothing attractive, and for their comfort – how false a comfort! – they may rest assured there is no danger of their being required to take up their inheritance at present. Perhaps they will be left to go on sucking *things* dry, constantly missing the loveliness of them, until they come at last to loathe the lovely husks, turned to ugliness in their false imaginations. Loving but the body of Truth, even here they come to call it a lie, and break out in maudlin moaning over the illusions of life. The soul of Truth they have lost, because they never loved her. What may they not have to pass through, what purifying fires, before they can even behold her!

The notions of Christians, so called, concerning the state into which they suppose their friends to have entered, and which they speak of as a place of blessedness, are yet such as to justify the bitterness of their lamentation over them, and the heathenish doubt whether they shall know them again. Verily it were a wonder if they did! After a year or two of such a fate, they might well be unrecognizable! One is almost ashamed of writing about such follies. The nirvana is grandeur contrasted with their heaven. The early Christians might now and then plague Paul with a foolish question, the answer to which plagues us to this day; but was there ever one of them doubted he was going to find his friends again? It is a mere form of Protean unbelief. They believe, they say, that God is love; but they cannot quite believe that he does not make the love in which we are most like him, either a mockery or a torture. Little would any promise of heaven be to me if I might not hope to say, 'I am sorry; forgive me; let what I did in anger or in coldness be nothing, in the name of God and Jesus!' Many such words will pass, many a self-humiliation have place. The man or woman who is not ready to confess, who is not ready to pour out a heartful of regrets – can such a one be an inheritor of the light? It is the joy of a true heart of an heir of light, of a child of that God who loves an open soul – the joy of any man who hates the wrong the more because he has done it, to say, 'I was wrong; I am sorry' .... All that is needed to set the world right enough for me – and no empyrean heaven could be right for me without it – is, that I care for God as he cares for me; that my will and desires keep time and harmony with his music; that I have no thought that springs from myself apart from him; that my individuality have the freedom that belongs to it as born of his individuality, and be in no slavery to my body, or my ancestry, or my prejudices, or any impulse whatever from region unknown; that I be free by obedience to the law of my being, the live and live-making will by which life is life, and my life is myself. What springs from myself and not from God, is evil; it is a perversion of something of God's. Whatever is not of faith is sin; it is a stream cut off – a stream that cuts itself off from its source, and thinks to run on without it. But light is my inheritance through him whose life is the light of men, to wake in them the life of their father in heaven. Loved be the Lord who in himself generated that life which is the light of men![56]

THANKFUL IN THE END

'You saved my life, Ian!' she said one evening for the tenth time.

'It pleased God you should live,' answered Ian.

'Then you really think,' she returned, 'that God interfered to save us?'

'No, I do not; I don't think he ever interferes .... Would you say a woman interfered in the management of her own house? Can one be said to interfere where he is always at work? He is the necessity of the universe, ever and always doing the best that can be done, and especially for the individual, for whose sake alone the cosmos exists. If we had been drowned, we should have given God thanks for saving us.'

'I do not understand you! .... How could we have thanked God for deliverance if we were drowned?'

'What! – not when we found ourselves above the water, safe and well, and more alive than ever? Would it not be a dreadful thing to lie tossed for centuries under the seawaves to which the torrent had borne us? Ah, how few believe in a life beyond, a larger life, more awake, more earnest, more joyous than this!'

' ... Then you must thank God for everything – thank him if you are drowned, or burnt, or anything!'

'Now you understand me! That is precisely what I mean.'

'Then I can never be good, for I could never bring myself to that!'

'You cannot bring yourself to it; no one could. But we must come to it. I believe we shall all be brought to it.'

' ... Can you suppose that Jesus at any time could not thank his Father for sending him into the world?'

'You speak as if we and he were of the same kind!'

'He and we are so entirely of the same kind, that there is no bliss for him or for you or for me but in being the loving obedient child of the one Father.'[57]

A TRANSFORMING HOPE

A conversation between Rachel and her uncle,
both of whom are little people, 'dwarfs'.

It was nearly dark when they arrived again at the lodge. Rachel opened the gate for them. Without even a *thank you*, they rode out. She stood for a moment gazing after them through the dusk, then turned with a sigh, and went into the kitchen, where her uncle sat by the fire with a book in his hand.

'How I should like to be as well made as Miss Lingard!' she said, seating herself by the lamp that stood on the deal table. 'It *must* be a fine thing to be strong and tall, and able to look this way and that without turning all your body along with your head, like the old man that gathers the leeches in Wordsworth's poem. And what it must be to sit on a horse as she does! You should have seen her go flying like the very wind across the park! You would have thought she and her horse were cut out of the same piece. I'm dreadfully envious, uncle.'

'No, my child; I know you better than you do yourself. There is a great difference between *I wish I was* and *I should like to be* – as much as between a grumble and a prayer. To be content is not to be satisfied. No one ought to be satisfied with the imperfect. It is God's will that we should bear, and contentedly – because in hope, looking for the redemption of the body. And we know he has a ready servant who will one day set us free.'

'Yes uncle; I understand. You know I enjoy life: how could I help it and you with me? But I don't think I ever go through the churchyard without feeling a sort of triumph – "There's for you!" I say sometimes to the little crooked shadow that creeps along by my side across the graves – "*You'll* soon be caught and put inside!" But how am I to tell I mayn't be crooked in the next world as well as this? That's what troubles me at times. There might be some necessity for it, you know.'

'Then will there be patience to bear it there also; – that you may be sure of. But I do not fear. It were more likely that those who have not thanked God, but prided themselves, that they were beautiful in this world, should be crooked in the next. It would be like Dives and Lazarus, you know. But God does what is best for them as well as for us. We shall find one day that beauty and riches were the best things for those to whom they were given, as deformity and poverty were the best for us.'

'I wonder what sort of person I would have been if I had had a straight spine!' said Rachel, laughing.

'Hardly one so dear to your deformed uncle,' said her companion in ugliness.

'Then I'm glad I am as I am,' rejoined Rachel.

'This conscious individuality of ours,' said Polwarth, after a thoughtful silence, 'is to me an awful thing – the one thing that seems in humanity like the onliness of God. Mine terrifies me sometimes – looking a stranger to me – a limiting of myself a breaking in upon my existence – like a volcanic outburst into the blue Sicilian air. When it thus manifests itself, I find no refuge but the offering of it back to him who thought it worth making. I say to him, "Lord, it is thine, not mine; see to it, Lord. Thou and thy eternity are mine, Father of Jesus Christ".'

He covered his eyes with his hands, and his lips grew white and trembled. Thought had turned into prayer, and both were silent for a space. Rachel was the first to speak. 'I think I understand, uncle,' she said. 'I don't mind being God's dwarf. But I would rather be made after his own image: this can't be it. I should like to be made over again.'

'And if the hope we are saved by be no mockery, if St Paul was not the fool of his own radiant imaginings, you will be, my child. But now let us forget our miserable bodies. Come up to my room, and I will read you a few lines that came to me this morning in the park.'

'Won't you wait for Mr Wingfold, uncle? He will be here yet, I think. It can't be ten o'clock yet. He always looks in on Saturdays as he goes home from his walk. I should like you to read them to him too. They will do him good, I know.'

'I would, my dear, willingly, if I thought he would care for them. But I don't think he would. They are not good enough verses. He has been brought up on Horace, and I fear counts the best poetry the neatest.'

'I think you must be mistaken there, uncle; I have heard him talk delightfully about poetry.'

'You must excuse me if I am shy of reading my poor work to any but yourself, Rachel. My heart was so much in it, and the subject is so sacred – '

'I am sorry you should think your pearls too good to cast before Mr. Wingfold, uncle,' said Rachel, with a touch of disappointed temper.

'Nay, nay, child!' returned Polwarth, 'that was not a good thing to say. What gives me concern is that there is so much of the rough dirty shell sticking about them, that to show them would be to wrong the truth in them.'

Rachel seldom took long to repent. She came slowly to her uncle, where he stood with the lamp in his hand, looking in his face with a heavenly contrition, and saying nothing – When she reached him, she dropped on her knees and kissed the hand that hung by his side. Her temper was poor Rachel's one sore-felt trouble.

Polwarth stooped and kissed her on the forehead, raised her, and leading her to the stair, stood aside to let her go first. But when she had been naughty Rachel would never go before her uncle, and she drew back. With a smile of intelligence he yielded and led the way. But ere they had climbed to the top, Rachel heard Mr Wingfold's step, and went down again to receive him.[58]

Looking away from Ourselves to Jesus and to Others

After a serious fever had broken, a seriously ill mother is concerned for the care of her son.

'I can even think of *him* now,' said the mother, 'without going into a passion. I hope God will forgive him. *I* do. I think He will forgive me.'

'Did you ever hear,' I asked, 'of Jesus refusing anybody that wanted kindness from Him? He wouldn't always do exactly what they asked Him, because that would sometimes be of no use, and sometimes would even be wrong; but He never pushed them away from Him, never repulsed their approach to Him. For the sake of His disciples, He made the Syrophoenician woman suffer a little while, but only to give her such praise afterwards and such a granting of her prayer as is just wonderful.'

She said nothing for a little while; then murmured, 'Shall I have to be ashamed to all eternity? I do not want not to be ashamed; but shall I never be able to be like other people – in heaven I mean?'

'If He is satisfied with you, you need not think anything more about yourself. If He lets you once kiss His feet, you won't care to think about other people's opinion of you even in heaven. But things will go very differently there from here. For everybody there will be more or less ashamed of himself, and will think worse of himself than he does of any one else. If trouble about your past life were to show itself on your face there, they would all run to comfort you, trying to make the best of it, and telling you that you must think about yourself as He thinks about you; for what He thinks is the rule, because it is the infallible right way. But perhaps rather, they would tell you to leave that to Him who has taken away our sins, and not trouble yourself any more about it. But to tell the truth, I don't think such thoughts will come to you at all when once you have seen the face of Jesus Christ. You will be so filled with His glory and goodness and grace, that you will just live in Him and not in yourself at all.'

'Will He let us tell Him anything we please?'

'He lets you do that now: surely He will not be less our God, our friend there.'

'Oh, I don't mind how soon He takes me now! Only there's that poor child that I've behaved so badly to! I wish I could take him with me. I have no time to make it up to him here.'

'You must wait till he comes. He won't think hardly of you. There's no fear of that.'

'What will become of him, though? I can't bear the idea of burdening my father with him.'

'Your father will be glad to have him, I know. He will feel it a privilege to do something for your sake. But the boy will do him good. If he does not want him, I will take him myself.'

'Oh! thank you, thank you, sir.' A burst of tears followed.

'He has often done me good,' I said.

'Who, sir? My father?'

'No. Your son.'

'I don't quite understand what you mean, sir.'

'I mean just what I say. The words and behaviour of your lovely boy have both roused and comforted my heart again and again.'

She burst again into tears.

'That is good to hear. To think of your saying that! The poor little innocent! Then it isn't all punishment?'

'If it were all punishment, we should perish utterly. He is your punishment; but look in what a lovely loving form your punishment has come, and say whether God has been good to you or not.'

'If I had only received my punishment humbly, things would have been very different now. But I do take it – at least I want to take it – just as He would have me take it. I will bear anything He likes. I suppose I must die.'

'I think He means you to die now. You are ready for it now, I think. You have wanted to die for a long time; but you were not ready for it before.'

'And now I want to live for my boy. But His will be done.'

'Amen. There is no such prayer in the universe as that. It means everything best and most beautiful, Thy will, O God, evermore be done.'

She lay silent. A tap came to the chamber-door. It was Mary, who nursed her sister and attended to the shop.

'If you please, sir, here's a little girl come to say that Mrs Tomkins is dying, and wants to see you.'

'Then I must say good-night to you, Catherine. I will see you to-morrow morning. Think about old Mrs Tomkins; she's a good old soul; and when you find your heart drawn to her in the trouble of death, then lift it up to God for her, that He will please to comfort and support her, and make her happier than health – stronger than strength, taking off the old worn garment of her body, and putting upon her the garment of salvation, which will be a grand new body, like that the Saviour had when He rose again.'

'I will try. I will think about her.'

For I thought this would be a help to prepare her for her own death. In thinking lovingly about others, we think healthily about ourselves. And the things she thought of for the comfort of Mrs Tomkins, would return to comfort herself in the prospect of her own end, when perhaps she might not be able to think them out for herself.[59]

END NOTES

1   *Unspoken Sermons,* Series 3: 'Creation in Christ', pp 8-10 (hereafter '*US*'.)

2   *US*, Series 1: 'The Hands of the Father', pp 186-188.

3   *US*, Series 1: 'The Child in the Midst', pp 17-22.

4   *US*, Series 1: 'The Child in the Midst', pp 22-26.

5   *US*, Series 1: 'The Consuming Fire', pp 27-28.

6   *Donal Grant:* chap LXII, pp 311-312.

7   *Guild Court: A London Story:* chap XLVI, pp 330-331.

8   *David Elginbrod:* chap XXII, pp 399-400.

9   *The Hope of the Gospel:* 'Salvation from Sin', pp 1-9.

10   *The Miracles of Our Lord,* 'The Raising of the Dead', pp 195-197.

11   *US*, Series 3: 'Freedom', pp 94-97.

12   *The Seaboard Parish:* chap XL, pp 580-581.

13   *Salted with Fire:* chap XVII, pp 163-167.

14   *US*, Series 3: 'Creation in Christ', pp 16-17.

15   *US*, Series 2: 'The Way', pp 3-6.

16   *US*, Series 2: 'Life', pp 142-144.

17   *US*, Series 3: 'Creation in Christ', pp 18-20.

18   *The Marquis of Lossie,* chap XLII, pp 192-194.

19   *US*, Series 3: 'Creation in Christ', pp 20-22.

20   *US*, Series 2: 'Abba Father', pp 122-126.

21   *US*, Series 2: 'The Last Farthing', pp 101-105.

22   *Paul Faber, Surgeon:* chap XXXII, p 231.

23   *Ranald Bannerman's Boyhood,* chap XXXII, pp 289, 296-299, 301.

24   *David Elginbrod:* chap XV, p 354.

25   *US*, Series 2: 'The Truth in Jesus', pp 242-246.

26   *US*, Series 1: 'The Higher Faith', pp 51-54.

27   *US*, Series 1: 'The Higher Faith', pp 59-61.

28   *Thomas Wingfold:* chap XXXVI, p 178-181.

29   *Saint George and Saint Michael:* chap LVI, p 421.

30   *Thomas Wingfold:* chap XVIII, pp 86-89.

31   *The Hope of the Gospel:* 'God's Family', pp 115-120.

32   *US*, Series 3: 'Creation in Christ', p 13-16.

33   *US*, Series 2: 'Life', pp 145-149.

34   *Mary Marston:* chap XI, pp 97-99.

35   *What's Mine is Mine:* chap X, pp 71-72.

36   *Thomas Wingfold:* chap XLV, pp 230-234.

37   *US*, Series 1: 'Love Thy Neighbour', pp 190-197.

38   'Divine and Human Relationship', *God's Words to His Children, Sermons Spoken and Unspoken* (New York: Funk & Wagnals, 1887). The editor of this collection is unknown.

39   *US*, Series 1: 'Love Thine Enemy', pp 219-224.

40   *Ranald Bannerman's Boyhood:* chap XVIII, pp 157-158.

41   *The Vicar's Daughter:* chap XXX, p 238.

42   *The Flight of the Shadow:* chap V, pp 43-44.

43   *US*, Series 3: 'The Mirrors of the Lord', pp 49-54.

44   *US*, Series 2: 'Self Denial', pp 225-227.

45   *US*, Series 2: 'The Word of Jesus on Prayer', pp 58-60.

46   *US*, Series 2: 'The Word of Jesus on Prayer', pp 72-74.

47   *The Hope of the Gospel:* 'Sorrow the Pledge of Joy, pp 97-100.

48   *The Seaboard Parish:* chap VIII, pp 92, 93-94.

49   *Thomas Wingfold, Curate:* chap XXXIX, pp 196-198.

50   *The Hope of the Gospel:* 'The Hope of the Universe', pp 205-207; 209-214.

51   *England's Antiphon: A Historical Review of the Religious Poetry of England* (MacMillan & Co Pub: n.d., p 279).

52   *US*, Series 2: 'The Voice of Job', p 196.

53   *Ranald Bannerman's Boyhood:* chap XV, p 130.

54   *US*, Series 3: 'The Knowing of the Son', pp 31-32.

55   *The Miracles of Our Lord:* 'Introduction', pp 3-7.

56   *US*, Series 3: 'The Inheritance', pp 255-262.

57   *What's Mine is Mine:* chap XXXI, pp 234-235.

58   *Thomas Wingfold, Curate:* chap XXXIV, pp 166-169.

59   *Annals of a Quiet Neighbourhood:* chap XXVIII, pp 492-495.